Not My Business

HOW I GAVE MY COMPANY TO GOD AND WHAT HAPPENED NEXT

Mark Beamish
with Dave Franco

Not My Business
Copyright © 2017 Mark Beamish
LinkBookLegacies.com
San Diego, California
All rights reserved.

As told by Mark Beamish
Written by Dave Franco
Cover Art Design Derek Wetter
Layout and Design Nichole Gagliardo

ISBN-13: 978-1974480852
Copyright Office Date of registration 8/24/2017 case number 1-5751416991

Some names and details of actual events have been changed to protect the identities of the persons involved.

All rights reserved. No portion of this publication may be reproduced, stored in a retrieval system, or transmitted in any form by any means—electronic, mechanical, photocopying recording or any other—except for brief quotations in printed reviews, without the prior permission of the publisher.

Scripture quotations taken from The Holy Bible, New International Version® NIV®
Copyright © 1973 1978 1984 2011 by Biblica, Inc. TM
Used by permission. All rights reserved worldwide.
Scripture quotations are from the ESV® Bible (The Holy Bible, English Standard Version®), copyright © 2001 by Crossway, a publishing ministry of Good News Publishers. Used by permission. All rights reserved.
Scripture quotations taken from the New American Standard Bible® (NASB),
Copyright © 1960, 1962, 1963, 1968, 1971, 1972, 1973,
1975, 1977, 1995 by The Lockman Foundation
Used by permission. www.Lockman.org
Scripture taken from the New King James Version®. Copyright © 1982 by Thomas Nelson.
Used by permission. All rights reserved.
Scripture quotations are taken from *The Living Bible* copyright © 1971. Used by permission of Tyndale House Publishers, Inc., Carol Stream, Illinois 60188. All rights reserved.

Printed in the United States of America.

TO MY WIFE, MY PARTNER IN ALL THINGS FROM THE BEGINNING.

Contents

Preface	7
Introduction	9
Chick, Vin and Ron	19
Whose Money it Really is	33
Gary	43
The Hand Off, Part 1	53
The Hand Off, Part II	63
Being Bill	73
My Answer	81
The Adrenaline Rush	95
The Banquet	121
Visitor to the Palace	131
Wink and a Nod	139
Three in the Pocket	149
The Close One	159
Footsteps	177
Epilogue	191

Preface

MY REASON FOR WRITING THESE STORIES from my life is because I have been blessed with much success and the journey is quite unique. The difference in my story from other books you may read where business is the focus is how I got here and what it all means. How I got here is a miracle, and what it all means, well, that's a miracle, too. You can follow in my footsteps, but this book is not a how-to. Rather, it's more like a who-to. It's all about to whom you give your heart, your business, and your wealth. It's not a formula for riches, as in money, but a formula for riches, as in a peace that passes all understanding. And that is what your heart wants most, whether *peace that passes all understanding* has made it to your list of life or business goals or not.

Introduction

I WALKED INTO THE APARTMENT that I shared with my wife, Karen, and looked around. It was strangely quiet. It was around 6:30 p.m. and she should have been home from work. When I turned the corner, she was there, standing in the kitchen with a look on her face that said she was not exactly happy to see me. We were newly-weds. This hadn't happened before.

"Hi. Everything alright?" I asked.

Everything was not alright.

Karen, who was just 20 years old, held down a full-time job while I, well, didn't. You see, I'd had jobs before, but between working and playing, working just didn't compare. Work wasn't near as fun, nor did it offer anywhere near the laughs. What's more, depending on the kind of job you had, it was generally very hard to get a good tan.

So, I would get up each day and get myself to the beach to spend the morning surfing with buddies. Then, we would go out to eat breakfast. My friends didn't have a lot of money, so I would often treat. Sometimes, if we were quick about it, we could hit the earliest showing of a movie, which was really great. Of course, there is lunch and softball and the gym to round out the day, after which, I would arrive home feeling pretty tuckered out. Sure, it was expensive, but Karen was working and bringing in pretty good money.

The problem arose when a family friend, a realtor who had seen "the perfect starter house" for us at a great price, called her that afternoon. Karen wanted out of our tiny apartment and was excited by the possibility—until she checked our savings account to see if we had enough to make the small down payment.

We didn't.

But, here's the worst part: The withdrawal records led directly to me. Karen had been making regular deposits and knew what the total should have been, but I had been making withdrawals a couple times a week for over a year. What happened next was a dressing down that I never saw coming. It was awful.

"I've never had to think about stuff like responsibility before—I mean, not like this," I told her as I tried to do a little blame shifting to my mother.

"Well, I'm not going to live this way," she said. "I've been working and saving money for our future and now I think I might have made a mistake by marrying you."

INTRODUCTION

It shook me to my core. I loved Karen very much. I couldn't have her feeling this way about me.

Determined to not let her down again, I took any job I could, from taking pictures of homes for an insurance salesman at five bucks a shot, to working the graveyard shift at a 7-Eleven. After a couple of months behind the counter of our local 7-Eleven, a man walked in with a gun and robbed me at gunpoint for the contents of the cash register. If that wasn't bad enough, on another night, an old high school classmate walked in and robbed me of my dignity.

"Mark Beamish?" my old classmate exclaimed. "You're working at a 7-Eleven? I thought you would be off doing great things—but you're working graveyard at a 7-Eleven? Man, I'm even doing better than you."

It was devastating. Between Karen's disappointment and my classmate's aghast at my incredible wasted life, I never felt so low.

I called an old friend, Sam, whose dad I worked for just after high school and asked if I could work with him once again. Sam agreed, but now he had his own waterproofing company. I was in.

It was a perfect fit. I made steady money and found myself feeling good about pulling my weight and reaching a level of respectability. I was quick and thorough on the job and liked physical work under the sun, which gave me one heck of a tan.

One afternoon, I was talking with a supplier who I had come to respect for being a sincere, stand-up guy.

"I don't see why you couldn't be getting your own jobs, just like Sam is doing," he said. "All you have to do is take some classes, get a license and you can start bidding." I had never thought of that before.

"That sounds like a great idea," I told him. In fact, it was such a great idea I walked into Sam's office and told him about my new plan. He fired me on the spot.

> It was there, high up on a ladder, that something in me began to change.

Suddenly unemployed again, I got a job with one of Sam's competitors. It was there, high up on a ladder, that something in me began to change. I noticed that the caulking used on many of the joints was a different product from several of the others. I had never seen anything like that before. "This guy's not paying his bills," I thought to myself. "He's having to buy from different suppliers because nobody will sell to him twice." Then, I noticed that the owner was paying over 200% of what Sam was paying per gallon of caulking. "He's not on anyone's preferred client list," I thought.

Later that week, on payday, I noticed the guys who worked on the job with me knocked off at 10 or 11 a.m. and did not return. I left the site at 3 p.m. to grab my check and get to the bank, but there were insufficient funds to cash the checks—the accounts had been depleted. "He can't stay solvent," I said to myself. "Whatever way he is spending his money, he is not thinking of his company or employees first."

Suddenly, I noticed that my mind was operating in a way it hadn't before—as if it had shifted to a new way of caring about what was going on around me. It was new territory for me. I wrote my new thoughts down.

> *Pay your people first*
>
> *Pay them what they are worth (Colossians 4:1)*
>
> *Pay your bills on time*
>
> *Be respected by your suppliers so you will be a preferred client*

For the first time, I was starting to think less like a player and more like an employer.

Suddenly, my ambition grew. I finished my classes, took the state exam, and received my license. I began driving the freeways looking for cranes because wherever there were cranes there was work. I would go to the sites and leave a bid right on the back of my business card. With a handshake, I started getting jobs. I never turned anything down. My team of guys became a well-oiled machine as I pushed them for and exemplified hard work and efficiency.

When Sam got wind of my success, he offered to bring me back, make me a partner, and work under his company name. I agreed. I was still bringing in new clients, and suddenly our business began to explode. We were making money hand over fist. That's when our company culture began to take a bit of a turn.

Sam and his guys began to gamble their newfound riches on everything they could. Not particularly interested in that brand of fun, I only dabbled in it to stay part of the team. But soon, I found myself becoming a runner for the group, driving up to Las Vegas with a pile of money to place bets. One night after winning big on a series of bets, Sam convinced me to hide a box holding $10,000 so his wife wouldn't find it. It was crazy. I was hiding Sam's money so his wife wouldn't find it—in a place in my closet so my wife wouldn't find it.

It only went downhill from there. When one of our suppliers, a successful and savvy businessman offered his boat in Cabo San Lucas, Mexico, for Marlin fishing, I used it to reward three of our employees. On our way down to Cabo, they drank themselves into a sloppy, slobbering state. Arriving at the dock where the boat was, my guys stumbled onboard, and then one fell over the edge nearly getting caught in the propellers. A fight broke out which caused the boat's captain to pull a knife. It was already getting completely out of hand and we hadn't even left the dock.

When the captain kicked us off the boat, we walked into a bar where one of my guys promptly picked a fight with a local. The bartender looked at me and asked, "You with him?"

"Yeah," I answered sheepishly.

"If I were you," he said, "I'd get out of here. The federales are coming and if you're here when they arrive, you're all going to jail."

We dashed out the back door and made our way down to the

beach. And that's when it hit me. My life was a mess. I was gambling. I was running money. I was hiding money from Sam's wife, and even from my own. I was hanging out with guys who were out of control, getting in fights, and I was running from the Mexican police. I knew this couldn't go on.

As a teenager, I had given my life to Jesus Christ after watching Billy Graham on TV. It was time to treat my Savior with reverence and obedience for the gift of eternal life, and give up my blatant disregard. I fell to my knees and begged for forgiveness.

When I returned home, I was different. I told Sam that it was time to part ways. He consented. We met at a restaurant and sorted out our customers on the back of a paper placemat. We agreed that going forward, he would retain his customers and I would keep the ones that I had brought to the partnership.

I breathed a sigh of relief and felt good about the future. I knew that in an industry where unethical business practices were the norm, someone who played by the rules and was driven by honesty and integrity—not money, would stand out. I was ready to offer the industry something new.

Two days later, I received a document that stated Sam was taking me to court for trying to steal his clients, and the prosecution was using my own handwriting on the paper placemat as evidence of premeditation. It was another devastating blow.

At a family get-together, I mentioned the lawsuit I was now embroiled in and my sister-in-law said she knew a lawyer who was a "bulldog." When I called the lawyer, he assured me he was the kind that played hardball. I retained him immediately. And to think I almost didn't bother the family with my legal trouble.

At Sam's deposition, my attorney raked Sam over the coals, devastating his claim that I was stealing from him. In the end, it was less like a deposition, and more like a demolition. "You've got an excellent case against him," my attorney said, "and if you want it, you can win more than $100,000 in receivables that are rightfully yours. He doesn't stand a chance. But I would advise against it," he asserted. I was a little shocked.

"Look," he continued, "if you fight, it will take years to win, cost you a lot of money, and you'll alienate all your customers in the process. But if he's anything like he appears to be, and you're the kind of person you appear to be, you'll have all his clients in two years whether you are trying to get them or not."

I liked the way that sounded. I agreed not to engage any of Sam's current client list for two years, which turned out to be more difficult than I could have ever guessed as many of Sam's disgruntled clients began to ask me to do their jobs. I had gained a reputation for bringing a level of quality, craftsmanship and speed to the jobs that most hadn't seen before. In fact, general contractors were getting used to simply giving me the job and asking me to send them a bill. Nobody in the industry trusted anybody that much—yet they did with me.

But even with a young family to support, I still refused all offers to work with Sam's clients, despite some begging. I reasoned with them, explaining that to do otherwise would be to go against my word. It angered a lot of the builders and general contractors—but they were also very impressed.

And they remembered.

I spent the next two years pursuing my own jobs, focusing on new ways to streamline processes, and following the ethical guidelines that comported with integrity and obedience to God. And over the years, I continued to add to that original list:

Fulfill every promise

Fix any problem immediately

Win every job, and be worth it

Be honest, even if it is to your own detriment

If employees believe they are the best, they will act like it

Mark Beamish Waterproofing (MBW) grew exponentially, becoming one of the largest caulking/waterproofing companies in the West. And when the two years were up, more than 90% of Sam's clients became clients of MBW.

I haven't always been the perfect son, and I certainly haven't always been the perfect businessman. Actually, I have been far from it by the world's perspective. In fact, let me push that even further. I have conducted my business in a way that would make most business-minded people shudder and shake their heads in disbelief. But I have given my life and company to God, tried to do everything that I thought would please Him, and He has blessed me more than I deserve. That's what this book is about.

1

Chick, Vin and Ron

Three…Beamish with the ball in the corner…two…he stutter steps to the left…one…he launches a jump shot from 24… blaaaaaaaarrrrrr….he hits it! Beamish sinks the shot with no time left on the clock! And the Fabulous Forum goes wiiiiiild!

THERE IS NO WAY TO CONVEY how much sports announcers Chick Hearn, of the Los Angeles Lakers, and Vin Scully of the LA Dodgers meant to me when I was a kid. I would emulate them while playing by myself, whether I was on a court or baseball field, or shooting a wadded up piece of paper into a trashcan. My life had a running play-by-play because the images those guys created in my head were so strong and exciting. I wanted to step inside that feeling as often as I could.

Two outs, bottom of the 9th, and who should come to the plate, but Mark Beamish! (Crowd roars). Beamish steps up as the crowd

NOT MY BUSINESS

stands to its feet. Here's the pitch. Beamish hits a deep fly ball to right, way back, waaaaay back—it's gone!

I consumed everything about sports—I absolutely loved it. The competition, the colors, the amazing plays and the legendary players, like Sandy Koufax, Jerry West, Maury Wills, Wilt Chamberlin, Willie Davis, Gail Goodrich. That's where my mind floated throughout the day. Of course, with sports on my mind all the time, it meant that other things in my life got no attention—work being top among them.

I hated work.

I would do anything to skip out of having to clean or lift or sweat my rear off in the sun, digging or clipping, or what have you. It didn't matter if my mom floated a few bucks in front of me to work, I still hated it—money never added much in the way of incentive. That is why it was all the more maddening the day she came home with a brilliant idea. My brothers, John, Paul and I were going to mow the lawns of our neighbors just because their entire family worked at their family restaurant, Mr. Rib—and they didn't have the time to do their own yard work. Mom felt that we needed to help them. And, we were going to get paid zero dollars. Can you believe that? We would get nothing?

So, there we were, out in the hot sun, mowing, edging, clipping, moving stuff around, picking up dog poop, and working ourselves to the bone. I hated every minute of it.

As I got a little older, you'd think I would mature into accepting that work was part of life, but I didn't. When John got a job working at Mr. Rib, he climbed right up the ranks and ended up being a cook. When I started working there, I washed dishes and that's where I stayed. They knew a guy who hated his job when they saw one.

Then, John got a job at a butcher shop and asked the owner to hire me. It was awful, dirty, sweaty work and I was miserable. Later, I worked for an older couple who owned the chicken place next door. That sucked too. I had always heard that work was good for you, but I didn't see it.

All I really wanted to do was play sports. My only other interest was girls, but I had an awful time talking to them. So, when I hung out with my buddies, we used to scrounge around for alcohol in their parents' cabinets or get it from their older siblings. We even did the "derelict-in-front-of-the-liquor-store" routine, where we'd ask dudes who were over 21 to buy us some beer. That seemed to work pretty well. The problem was, I hated beer. But, if I was ever going to get the courage to talk to girls, I had to drink.

When I came across pot in high school, however, everything changed. I loved it. I couldn't get enough. Friends would share theirs with me until I started smoking so much that they pointed out the sellers around our campus at Bolsa Grande High, and told me to have at it. I bought and got high every day.

This was about the time my dad passed away. Getting high was a good distraction from all of that. And so, I would surf in the morning, get to school by 10 or 11 a.m., and write my own excuse note. Then, I would get high after school with buddies. Where before I was a decent student suddenly my grades tanked. I was basically an addict and when one is, everything in life begins to loosen to the point of falling apart. That's what happened to me. I got careless about how and where I bought pot. Sure enough, I got arrested along with my stoner friends and we were hauled off to jail.

My mom was convinced that my friends were bad influences and I let her go right on thinking that. But the truth was, I was the bad influence. I had become the ringleader.

My brother, Paul, took a job at the Army Navy Surplus store in Westminster, and then I did too. I worked the back warehouse sweeping, straightening and keeping inventory. Of course, I hated it. But then, I realized that nobody really checked on me, or what I was doing. I was such a work-hating burnout by this point, I figured that if I got some sleeping bags and blankets together, climbed up on a little loft and fell asleep, who was going to know?

> When I came across pot in high school, everything changed.

So, that is what I did. Day after day after day, I would arrive at work, go up to the loft, get high, snuggle up and fall asleep for hours. Nobody said a word. One night I woke up and it was pitch black. I didn't have a clue as to what time it was, or how long I had been up there. Was it midnight? I was like, "Oh crap. I have a date!"

So, I jumped down from the loft and tried to find my way to the big sliding door that separated the front part of the store from the back. I found it, but couldn't open it. I was locked in. I began to freak out. I started slamming my fist against the door and screaming to see if I could get the attention of anybody who might be passing by on the outside of the store. I was going ballistic.

Suddenly, the door opened up and the guys who worked on the other side of the store were there. It was only 9:02 p.m.—two minutes after closing.

"Dude, calm down," they said, looking at me like I was losing it. "You're making a scene." They were right. I was.

It was about this time that I began to realize that I probably couldn't go on this way. My work ethic was a disaster. My dad had died, and therefore, was not around to be of any guidance—and never really was, actually. He worked so much I hardly ever saw him. I had no direction. I was smoking pot like crazy. How was I going to end up? What kind of person would I become? I didn't know it then, but I was smack dab in the middle of a pivotal time—and my life was about to experience a tidal shift.

Walt Hoffman, the father of two friends of mine, had been sharing the Gospel with me in one form or another ever since he was my Pop Warner football coach. Initially, I was fairly put off by the whole Christian thing, largely based on the kinds of people I knew who were Christians—nerdy guys with short hair and skinny ties. But, when I would go over to the Hoffman's house for a Bible study, there were some cool guys there who were "full-on Christians." It made an impression on me. Still, I wasn't quite sure about it and kept my distance. The problem was that Christianity began to mess with my conscience. In fact, I was in such a state of confusion that the girl I was dating, the hottest girl around, kept wondering when I was going to make a move on her body. I was really conflicted. I knew that the God Walt spoke of had very good reasons why I shouldn't do it. So, I kept putting it off, which was something that I hadn't done with other girls up to that point, especially when given such an opportunity. Finally, her friend came up to me and said that my girlfriend thought I might be gay. She was so chased-after by all the guys, I could certainly understand her point of view. Nobody turns down someone like her unless something out of the ordinary was happening on the inside. And for me, it certainly was.

Meanwhile, Gary and Jim, two buddies of mine from school, worked for a guy named Sam, whose dad owned a construction company. I got a job with them in the summer of 1974 attracted by two things—the opportunity to make as much money as Gary and Jim—who in my mind were rich—and to work for an older dude. Maybe he could help fill the ache in my heart from not having a dad.

It was another life-changing moment.

The culture of work that existed between Gary and Jim was unlike anything I had ever seen before. These two guys were so competitive that everything was a contest. From who could climb the ladders the fastest, to who could get the most work done, to who could toss the most toothpicks into a tray at lunch. And they weren't just whatever about it. They had rules of engagement they took very seriously. It was never simply toothpicks to them. Serious bragging rights were always on the line.

All of a sudden, I found myself having to keep up—or else I would be their whipping boy. So, I jumped in and tried to win at everything, and at all cost. Where before I was the guy who was only good for spending eight hours of company time sleeping away a pot-induced stupor, now I was hustling—even dashing through every shift—and I was having more fun than ever. I was learning what my body could do in terms of how *hard* I could work. I was also about to learn how *good* I could work.

> Maybe he could help fill the ache in my heart from not having a dad.

Ron Reed couldn't have been taller than 5'6." Part general contractor and part General Bonaparte, he was a small guy with a gigantic presence on our job sites. He was a construction supervisor who walked the dusty pathways between buildings, wore pleated pants, pressed shirts, and had perfectly combed hair. He was uncommonly comfortable in his own skin, fully committed to doing excellent, detail-oriented work no matter that his job sites were swarming with filthy, coarse, beer-drinking men who were looking to get done and home as fast as possible. Ron would take you to task no matter who you were, even if you were a seen-it-all, 30-year construction veteran. He didn't care. You either did the job right, or you were out. Everybody hated working with him. To them, he was a self-absorbed blowhard in the wrong business. We were making buildings, after all. Not cakes.

When he would get on my case and tell me how he needed the work to be just so, I would bite my tongue, but I would think to myself, *C'mon, dude. You're ridiculous. Everything you're asking for is a complete joke.*

One day, he called me over to a wall that I had just caulked. I thought, *Oh, great, here we go again.* He pointed to the bottom of the joint. I expected him to complain, but to my surprise, he got personal.

"Why did you do it this way?" he asked earnestly. He said it in a way that seemed to really be asking, *What kind of person are you?*

I had to stop and think about it. I wasn't prepared to ask myself what it was inside that made me care so little about something I was getting paid to care about a lot. If the job wasn't done well, why was I willing to consider it finished just because *nobody was ever going to notice?*

What kind of person was I?

"Spend the time to do the job right the first time," he said, "and you'll actually save time because you won't have to go back and correct your mistakes later like you're going to do now."

He began to show me how he wanted it done, a method and ideology that, if followed, would add about 25% more time to each job and seemingly result in little, if any, benefit.

But then I started to understand him. If *I* were to do the joints perfectly, I would *be* better for it, and I would *feel* better *for* it, because I would have pride in my work knowing that the bottom of the joint was done to perfection—even if nobody would ever see it. In fact, I would feel better *because* no one would see it. It was like my little deal with myself. I was creating beauty just for beauty's sake. It struck a chord with me. I wanted to feel that way. My respect for Ron suddenly rocketed. He was an older guy, a father figure, who cared enough to make me a better person.

Everything changed. I began to feel a sense of pride in my work that I had never felt before. Suddenly, having the most perfectly executed joints with the cleanest job area meant everything to me. And he was right. The more I treated my caulking like an art, the more pride I would have and the better I would feel. I was becoming a different person.

But Ron wasn't finished with me. Without him even knowing it, he helped me become a better Christian, too.

By this time, I had fully stepped into the faith. I had given my heart to Christ and really took it on. By pushing me towards excellence in all things, he provided clarity on how I was living out my faith. I could suddenly see how lax I was in my Christian walk when no one was around to notice my actions. He showed me that a man was someone who was the same when he was alone as when he was with other people. In some circles, I believe they call this *integrity*.

Ron had always said, "Do the job right, and you and I will get along just fine." That turned out to be very true. After a while, he stopped giving me a hard time about my work and we started having very nice conversations. He would tell me about his wife and kids, and how he loved to take them dirt biking, and the joys of family—things that had to do with life. Then he would start to request me on his jobs. I could not have been more flattered. I wanted to work for Ron because he made me feel good about myself. What greater gift can you ask for?

Later, when I had my own company, everything that I learned from Ron began to bloom. I spoke his truths as if they originated from me—but I knew they hadn't. They were Ron's wisdom and characteristics that I had emulated, and they became a part of me. I would hire young guys to come out and learn how to be a part of a caulking team, and all the finer points. I would show them how to do it, with all my specific requirements—and I would watch their eyes. If they thought my instruction on how to load a gun, or hand a gun to the caulker, or whatever it was, was ridiculous—and they rolled their eyes, they had just taken a step toward the door. If they kept it up, they would be fired, no questions asked. Caulking is an art. It may not look like it, but it is. Every job is an art. And if they couldn't see it, they could do a shoddy job for someone else. It was Ron's temperament to a T.

My experience with Ron was the beginning of what my reputation would become years later when Mark Beamish Waterproofing was getting up and running. Just like Chick or Vin when I was a kid, I carried Ron's voice with me at all times. I followed Ron in nearly every way—even the way he looked, to a certain degree. He gave me the license to be rather tidy on the job site, just like he was, without a speck of dirt on me. We did meticulous work and I pushed my employees for ever-increasing excellence and care for their performance and efficiency. Builders from all around began to notice, and that reputation has meant everything to me. It built a great company. It helped me employ and provide a very nice living for hundreds of people. It means God used me and MBW to give people sustenance, homes, educations, vacations, weddings, and the list goes on and on.

Ron Reed, wherever you are, I can't begin to thank you enough.

FOR REFLECTION

In handing my life over to Christ, I began to see that He was slowly changing me. Where once I hated work, I now started to take pride in what I was doing. Instead of running or hiding from work, I found myself wanting to be on the job from sun up to sun down. Do you love your work, or do you harbor resentment for having to be on the job? If you saw work as less of a paycheck and more of an opportunity to please God, how would your work change?

Colossians 3:22-24 says, "Slaves, obey your earthly masters in everything; and do it, not only when their eye is on you and to curry their favor, but with sincerity of heart and reverence for the Lord. Whatever you do, work at it with all your heart, as working for the Lord, not for human masters, since you know that you will receive an inheritance from the Lord as a reward. It is the Lord Christ you are serving."

After I figured out that God didn't create me to hit a fastball or dunk a basketball, I realized He created me to caulk a great joint in a tilt up or build a great team of individuals into a dynamic company. What did God create you to be? What skills or talents did He place in you that perhaps, you have forgotten about? Are you using them to your greatest ability for His greatest glory? Ask Him to show you what it is.

2

Whose Money it Really is

HE IS ALL BOY. As my 7-year-old grandson, Chase, goes from toy to toy, he does so with a mischievous grin and reckless abandon. He likes crashing his toys, shoving down handfuls of food, jumping in the pool with arms and legs going in every direction and giving his little sister, Charlotte, a good yank. That's why it makes perfect sense to me that when he hears women saying things like, "Chase, with those darling blue eyes, and those beautiful long eyelashes, *you are so adorable*," it makes him cringe and those beautiful blue eyes roll.

I know exactly what he is going through. I see his blue eyes and long eyelashes every time I look in the mirror, and recall so vividly what it was like to have them as my calling card. I was called beautiful, handsome, gorgeous, or "the best looking guy anybody has ever seen" as far back as I can remember, and as a kid, like Chase, *I hated it*.

Over time, who I was and what I looked like became one and the same. I seemed to cause a stir wherever I went. Nobody seemed to meet me and not comment. At first, it was a nuisance, but after a while, I began to believe it. I thought I was special. The odd thing is, even to this day, I don't know if that isn't, to some degree, true. God makes some people attractive, and He chose me. To boast about it seems vain, but to deny it and act like it isn't there seems silly. Because God blessed me with good looks, the door of opportunity opened and people wanted to work with me. It is through that blessing and others that MBW has had financial success, thereby providing me with the freedom to give to others with a grateful heart. Should I act like it isn't there? Should I refrain from giving God thanks?

It's a very uncomfortable topic—I'll be the first to tell you. No one likes to talk about their own attractiveness. Well, maybe some do, but I don't. And yet, if I were to list all the things that led to my success, leaving out that one aspect would be to turn a blind eye to God's intention and provision. Who am I to do that?

By the time I was a teenager, my understanding of what I brought to this world was clearly defined. I knew the power my appearance had because the effects of it were constantly playing out around me. In high school I was voted class president, and there wasn't one person in my school, myself included, that believed I won because of some achievement, vision or ability. There was one reason I won and one reason only.

Speaking of winning, I was on a 70s TV game show called the Dating Game, and won the big prize even though the girl who chose me could not see me. As it turns out, she didn't need to. There in the front row of the audience sat her three best friends all of whom emphatically held up two fingers to indicate that she should choose bachelor number two. Me. (The Dating Game was a TV show where a young woman asks questions of three bachelors she cannot see in order to select one for a date).

Even so, I still had a hard time talking to girls. But if I could just get some beer in me and settle down, I knew the rest was automatic. Yes, I took advantage of it, and I am not proud of that at all. I felt horrible for what I was doing and I know I hurt a lot of girls in the process. It was incredibly empty for all concerned.

Even after hitting some hard times, when I was at my most directionless, I felt like I was meant for something more. My history as someone who always believed I was special—because I was treated as such—propelled me to feel that way. But then the Gospel message of Jesus Christ came into my life at age 18, and once I found out that He died for me on the cross just so that we could spend eternity together, it was an affirmation—because Jesus died to save *me*. If there was ever any possibility that my self-worth would tank, that was gone forever. I gave my heart and my life to Jesus and I have never looked back. Between how God made me, and how He saved me, I knew good things were ahead.

And so, once I learned some very valuable lessons from Ron Reed, including that it was okay to be groomed on a construction site, I felt good about being my neat, slightly coiffed self. I worked that way every day. I didn't know it at the time, but I was bringing all my God-given physical attributes together to make a brand for myself that was more potent than I could have ever imagined.

Prior to getting into caulking, I tried my luck as a life insurance salesman. I thought that to be squeaky clean and wear a suit and tie was the sharpest, most respectable way a man could show up for work. And besides, I really liked how I looked in a suit. But soon, I figured out that I hated selling insurance. So, once I found myself working on construction sites with guys in the dirtiest clothes imaginable, I had to figure out how to feel good about myself regardless of the filthy conditions. I began to take my shirt off and wear shorts in order to get as much sun as possible—the goal being to turn myself into the darkest white guy around. As a surfer, this seemed to fit the image perfectly—and I felt good about that. In fact, instead of scheduling our jobs to be in the shade throughout the day, I worked in reverse, when the sun was most intense.

In addition, I was obnoxiously impeccable. I didn't like to get any of the caulking on me, the ladders or the trucks. If any of the caulking did get on me, I would remove it immediately. So there, on these pigsty construction sites, was this clean, bronzed surfer with long brown hair, no shirt, big blue eyes and long eyelashes, in perfectly pristine dolphin shorts (yes, I know, bad mental picture), flying up and down the ladders in the sun like a caulking superhero. Talk about making an impression. I don't think the general contractors or other workers had ever seen anything like it. I started to get a name for myself: *Ojos Azul*.

But it wasn't just about me. I pushed my guys to keep the most spotless work sites imaginable. Most construction sites looked like a tornado hit them. Not ours. Everything was neat. All trash was gathered and thrown away. In addition, I wanted our trucks to be spic and span—a clean and neat fleet.

Add all that up, and builders were more than intrigued. The MBW image generated the interest, which translated to new accounts and profits. God was undoubtedly blessing my life and he was using my image and appearance to do it. Of course, we had to deliver excellence, and we did. All the blue eyes in the world won't bring the customers back if you do a lousy job.

> God was blessing my life, and using my image and appearance to do it.

Now the question may be asked of me, *Why did God bless you with all of this?* I'm not sure I have *the* answer. But I can make this guess. Walt Hoffman, probably the most influential man in bringing me to Christ and someone to whom I am forever indebted, was a wealthy man who was quietly and graciously generous with everything he had. In his mind, what was his, was actually God's, and he gave of those finances freely. There were other men who attended Yorba Linda Friends who were of great means but were also insanely generous. They each had a profound effect on me.

When all the money in your account is actually owned by God, and not you, there is freedom—freedom to give, freedom to never feel the anxiety of a tightly-held fist, and freedom to receive with humility. Whenever I hear someone talk of how *they* acquired *their* riches, it makes me feel uncomfortable and sad for them. They have missed the boat entirely. They have all that money, yet they are slaves to their riches. So what good is it?

Not that I was never there myself. Earlier in my story, I told you about my time in Cabo San Lucas with my three fellow employees where we got in a fight, got kicked off the fishing boat by the captain, got into another fight in a bar, and then found ourselves running from the Mexican police. At that time, I was definitely of the mindset that my money was mine, that more is better, and that life was about acquiring. When I finally fell on my knees and asked for forgiveness, I found these words coming from my mouth: *I don't want all that, I only want You.* Everything changed that day—my heart and my business. The Bible is replete with Scripture confirming that "everything you have is God's." *See, Malachi 3:7-12.*

> We got in a fight, got kicked off the fishing boat by the captain, got into another fight in a bar, and then ran from the Mexican police.

In addition, Karen always tithed what little money we had in the early years with great ease and regularity. Her Quaker upbringing had instilled that in her. Between Walt, Karen and the generous men of Yorba Linda Friends, any thought about "my money" belonging to me imploded. I began to feel *great joy* about giving to our church as if that's what all of the money was actually for.

When our church started a capital campaign, Karen and I jumped in and helped out as much as we could, giving money and holding events at our house to help raise funds. Finally, the church exposed the fact that they were behind in their goals. Karen and I prayed about it, and then, with the stroke of a pen, we somehow committed to giving a sum of money that neither of us actually believed we could pull off. In fact, the sum was so large that the monthly installments far exceeded any other rent, mortgage or equipment payments we made.

In the first few months, we sweated it out. But over time, we could see that it was doable, and *it was God who was doing it*. He was performing a miracle through us, and growing our business by leaps and bounds. Perhaps God entrusted me with so much because He knew I would give it back?

One thing for sure, we were not responsible for the explosive success we experienced. We were two kids from Garden Grove with no business know-how or college degree between us. Only God could have orchestrated such a thing.

That is an indisputable fact.

People get mad at me when they think that I am saying the more money I give, the more I can expect to receive, as if it is some formula. I'm not saying that at all. My point is this: take your blessings—the strengths that God gave you, *even if it is your looks or image*, use them the best way you know how, and give freely to God what is His—which is everything. It may not be a formula for more riches, but it is a formula for more joy.

Joy.

Because if you want money so badly that you have to have it, you won't enjoy it if you ever get it.

MALACHI 3:7-12 (NIV)

7 Ever since the time of your ancestors you have turned away from my decrees and have not kept them. Return to me, and I will return to you," says the Lord Almighty.

"But you ask, 'How are we to return?'

8 "Will a mere mortal rob God? Yet you rob me.

"But you ask, 'How are we robbing you?'

"In tithes and offerings. 9 You are under a curse—your whole nation—because you are robbing me. 10 Bring the whole tithe into the storehouse that there may be food in my house. Test me in this," says the Lord Almighty, "and see if I will not throw open the floodgates of heaven and pour out so much blessing that there will not be room enough to store it. 11 I will prevent pests from devouring your crops, and the vines in your fields will not drop their fruit before it is ripe," says the Lord Almighty. 12 "Then all the nations will call you blessed, for yours will be a delightful land," says the Lord Almighty.

FOR REFLECTION

Ephesians 2:10 (ESV) says, "[for we are His workmanship, created in Christ Jesus for good works..."

At some point, I realized that God made me the way I was. Instead of holding on too tightly or taking credit for it, I praised and thanked Him and then gave it all back to Him by utilizing it for the Kingdom. How is your talent a throughway to increasing God's Kingdom?

Before I asked Jesus into my life, I used my looks in a way that was not pleasing to God. Are you misusing God's gift or not acknowledging His gift to you? Living for Him and using what He's blessed you with brings joy and freedom. If you are not experiencing that, why do you think that is?

3

Gary

THERE I WAS, HAVING JUST TAKEN THE SNAP FROM THE CENTER and moving quickly backward while the defense rushed me. My offensive line would fight to give me as much time as possible for making the pass—about four seconds, tops. What the defense didn't know is that they could rush me all they wanted. I had an ace in the hole. Gary Gutierrez was my wide receiver. He was so fast that all I would have to do is get that ball high and deep. Gary would fly underneath it like a heat-seeking missile. We connected with regularity, Gary and me. It's one of my favorite memories of those years: watching him with one of my passes tucked under his arm, running to daylight.

I met Gary when we were freshmen in high school, but when he became my go-to wide receiver the following year, we struck up a friendship. The fast-talking, faster running, knee-bouncing dude with enough energy to light a small city was my opposite. My whole vibe was laid back and cool. Gary's was to do everything in a blur.

> His brother was mean as a snake—the kind of guy who, if you just looked at him wrong, would be in your face, threatening your life.

We weren't best friends, but pals all the same. I always liked and respected Gary. He even served a good purpose. You see, his brother was as mean as a snake—the kind of guy who, if you just looked at him wrong, would be in your face, threatening your life. Everybody was scared to death of him, myself included. And while most guys experienced his wrath at one time or another, he was mostly mild around me. I think Gary ran interference, if you want to know the truth, telling him to leave me alone. Thank God for that.

Gary and I remained friends throughout high school. After, when I started attending Monday Night Bible Study (MNBS) at Alamitos Friends Church, where Karen and her family attended, Gary showed up after being invited by a girl who only came once, and never again. Once Gary saw how alive and exciting that Bible study was, he was hooked. That's when he started to hear Walt speak about the Good News of the Cross of Jesus Christ, and suddenly everything changed for him.

It was great to see.

Gary had a particularly tough upbringing. His dad was a fiery Mexican and his mom was short-fused and Irish, and the combination made for a hair-trigger life. His brother lived in a continuously agitated state and was prone to pushing back on all authority and conventional thinking. He got deeply into drugs and alcohol and ultimately spent much of his adult life whiling away his time strung out and living in places unknown.

Gary did drugs—so did I, for that matter—and was probably meant for a life similar to his brother. That is why it was all the more beautiful to see him have a chance at a wholesome, clean life there at MNBS with Walt, and tons of us guys. We bonded over reading the Bible, attending the study, going to church, surfing, playing sports, and doing life together. Gary dated, then married a very nice, soft-spoken girl who was a stabilizing force for him, and they began their journey together with the goal to serve God and do life right. Again, knowing where he was from and his chips-are-down beginning, it was so great to see him break the cycle. God had done a mighty work in his life.

When I took a job working for Sam's caulking company, Jim and Gary, who both went to MNBS, already worked there, and we found ourselves not only spending a lot of social time together, but working five eight-hour shifts a week shoulder-to-shoulder. I didn't mind it at all. Gary was a good guy and a great worker with a solid head on his shoulders. He made me better at what I did.

A few years later, after I told Sam I wanted to pursue my own license and he asked me to leave the company, I needed help. I asked Gary to come work with me. By this time, Gary had made a few questionable decisions in his life, including letting his marriage fail, and a lot of the Monday Nighters had given him a bit of the cold shoulder when he didn't toe the moral line like they advised him. As for me, I felt pretty certain that I was also a flawed character, like us all, and didn't see the need to hold anything against him. So, Gary and I were together again.

We were both hungry to make it, and for a time, we were really racking up accounts and putting up big numbers. All the successes allowed us to believe that perhaps we could be a partnership and work under my license. But, there was just one problem. We locked horns on nearly every decision. He was hardheaded about the things he believed in, and I was equally as stubborn. We were arguing daily and it was exhausting. I found myself beginning to contemplate the idea of cutting Gary loose from the business. Suddenly, and rather painfully, I knew it was what I had to do, and it was just a matter of picking the right time. The thought of cutting him off from his livelihood and his forward advance in life—with all our history—was agonizing. I had to trust that God would take care of him and that Gary's good workmanship would be recognized and rewarded by someone else. *Oh Lord, please.*

The day came that I was going to let him go and it was unbearable. I took him aside and told him that I thought it was better if I went in a different direction than where he wanted to go. Actually, exactly what I said is not clear to me. I think my mind has blocked out much of it. But just like that, it was over. He was hurt. I was hurt. It was awful.

> I felt pretty certain that I was also a flawed character, and didn't see the need to hold anything against him.

Some years later, after things at MBW were going great, I got a call from Gary. Previously, he had moved to Northern California with his new wife, bought a house and tried to develop his own business there. But the recession rolled through and hit him hard. He lost his house, his income and he was down to his last few bucks. So, he called me and asked if there was any work that I could offer him. I just happened to have a few jobs in Minden, Nevada, and I asked him to meet me there.

One night, while we were rooming together, I kept thinking about what had gone down between us years earlier and it was eating at me. Right then and there, I told him that the success I had with MBW and the way it blessed my family was something that should have happened to him, too. I didn't know when or how, but as soon as I could make it happen, I was going to try to help him get back to where he should have been if we hadn't parted ways. He was such a quality guy, it didn't seem right that I was working him for $20 an hour in the middle of a Nevada desert.

Besides, he was my friend.

About three and a half years later, times were tough for the business and it was looking like everybody in the company, including me, was going to have to take a cut in pay. One of my best guys, however, refused. I pushed the issue with him until finally, the pressure was just too much. He jumped ship to another company.

I replaced him with a new dude who ended up being able to do less than half of what I needed. Now with our company limping along, there was a hole that needed to be filled. Considering there was also a hole in my heart, why not kill two birds?

I called Gary. When I did, he was working for his dad, slogging away in a blazing Arizona quarry barely making ends meet. "Gary," I said, "how would you like to come and work for me?" I don't know what it felt like for him, but I know what it felt like for me. It was like jumping into a cool pool on a sweltering day.

Now here is the part of the story that is the reason why it is included in the pages of my life. Every Christian is endowed with the promise that, no matter how dire things get, a miracle is just around the corner. It can be a chance meeting, or a wrong turn, or a bolt of lightning…or a phone call away. That's the "hope" that Jesus gives all of us—that on this side of heaven, God can change our earthly circumstances in a moment's notice, and most often, when we least expect it. What a blessing it was that God used me to make good on that hope for Gary. MBW, a one-time little caulking company out of my garage, was now big and powerful enough to be *hope* for others.

Gary came to work for MBW, and along with alleviating the guilty ache that plagued me for so many years, it was a perfect match. We were great together, and business picked up once again. After a while, Gary and his wife wanted to return to Northern California to be with her mom after her dad died. Gary asked if he could start an office up there and I thought it sounded like a pretty good idea. So, we sent Gary to Auburn to start MBW North office, but for a lot of logistical reasons, it was having a hard time taking hold. Gary met a guy up there named Rich who he believed would be good for the business and could get them on track. He told me he wanted to hire him, but he wanted to pay him so much that I didn't see any way for both Rich and me to draw money from the business.

I let Gary hire him and agreed to take just a small amount so they could get up to speed and get going. Gary was right. Rich was very good for the business. They got some significant accounts and their operation moved forward with a full head of steam. Finally, I saw no reason why I shouldn't just back out altogether. I certainly didn't need what little was coming in. I deeded the business to Gary, and off they went—and they have never looked back.

Two decades later, Gary is still doing great. The business is bringing in millions of dollars per year, and he built a beautiful home in the mountains. Gary's wife is a lovely, smart person and such a compliment to Gary. They have beautiful, accomplished children who do exciting things like graduate from universities, become world-class skiers, and love and serve God. Gary is generous with what God has given him, and has provided for others in the name of Jesus. That is best of all.

I've been in Bible studies over the years where successful guys will harbor guilt over building businesses and not jumping into the trenches—on the mission fields—where the "real work" of reaching others for Christ is. I'm not sure that's correct. I think it's all real work. At least with the blessings I have received in my heart, it certainly feels like real work. I think Gary would agree.

I think back to those two crazy, lost kids who just "happened" to be on the same football team and find it amazing that God had such intent for bringing us together. It brings tears to my eyes that God was loving enough to give me the blessing of Mark Beamish Waterproofing, and allowed me to pass it to my friend Gary, who caught it, and all these years later, is still running to daylight.

FOR REFLECTION

Have you made decisions that haunt you, detrimentally changed the course of your life, or caused pain to others?

Romans 8:28 (NASB) says, "And we know that God causes all things to work together for good to those who love God, to those who are called according to His purpose."

Ask God to reveal how He might take a mistake that you have made and bring something good from it—even if years have past. Ultimately, God redeemed my decision to part ways with Gary, and the more I look, the more I see that He has done that many times throughout my life. Can you identify when God made good from something bad? If so, how can you thank Him for His faithfulness today?

4

The Hand Off, Part 1

THE TRIP TO CABO SAN LUCAS, when I realized how off-course my life had become, was at once horrifying and hopeful. I knew I was a mess, suddenly living in a way I never would have imagined. My sin had reached deep inside and suddenly, my spirit felt achy. It was as if my soul had the flu.

In reaching bottom, I called out to God in a way that I hadn't before. When I told Him I no longer wanted my will, but only His, I absolutely meant it from the deepest part of me. I was letting go of my life and turning everything over to Him—my business, my family, my future. I had felt the pain and shame of having lived a secret life, and now, I was done. It was over. On my knees with my hands raised, I let go and gave up.

Picture a cluster of helium balloons rising into the sky.

The feeling was so amazing that I knew I couldn't risk it to my own devices. I called Floyd Thorne, a friend from Monday Night Bible Study, who was both a bit older and someone I looked up to on matters of faith. Floyd came from a heavy drug and tough-guy background and had experienced an incredible transformation after surrendering to God. He had given everything to God and was rewarded with great faith, discipline, and freedom. I wanted that. I knew that if we rekindled our friendship and I revealed everything to him, I would stay steady on my new path of commitment. Floyd became my confessor.

> Karen and I had decided to relinquish everything to God, including our money.

As Floyd and I spent more and more time together, he invited Karen and me to attend a few Teen Challenge programs in support of his friend, Mike, who was trying to kick his heavy drug habit. At the events, we felt God's presence and could see that the work going on there was bearing a crazy amount of fruit. People were breaking loose from their heroin and cocaine addictions and stepping back into life as committed followers of Christ. It was really something to witness. Now that Karen and I had decided to relinquish everything to God, including our money, we wanted to step up and support Teen Challenge financially, so we did. We were all in. I attended various men's activities and programs, while Karen went to fashion shows and get-togethers, all sponsored by Teen Challenge. We were having a great time. Once we realized that our business and money belonged to God, life became incredibly fun.

When Mike was scheduled to graduate from Teen Challenge, we went to the ceremony. Afterward, everyone was standing around and introducing each other to family and friends, when suddenly I was introduced to a guy named Robert Mejia, the sight of whom was rather shocking. Robert, who was still in Teen Challenge, was a short, thick, powerful looking Mexican dude from the gangs and heroin scene of Santa Ana. He had cropped black hair and tattoos that climbed out from under his shirt, covered his neck and reached up to his face. But that wasn't the most amazing part. Robert wore a smile that was so broad, and filled with such joy, you couldn't help but be taken by him. The contrast between his tough guy look and his incredible love and gusto for Jesus Christ beaming from that smile was like a banner over his head that said, *Miraculously Changed Life.*

I knew that the requirement to graduate from Teen Challenge was to find employment, and it occurred to me that I could remedy that. I talked to Karen and she was all for it—so I offered Robert a job. He was happy, but I think I was even happier. I felt a certain letting go pulsing through my body and God confirming it yet again in my heart. *Yup*, He seemed to be saying. *It's all about Me.*

When Robert arrived on the job site, it was an exciting and anxious moment. How would this go? He was a gangbanger from the streets. Did he even have a work ethic? I was happy to give him a job for the sake of his progress, but he had to perform. My guys worked in teams. There could be no weak links.

Robert's build and experience didn't seem appropriate for risking him to the ladders, and the only job that seemed right for him was one of the dirtiest tasks on the site. I showed him what to do, sent him on his way and held my breath—but he performed on the job like he was made for it. In fact, he was a great worker. There was Robert, with his filthy, blackened skin providing the perfect backdrop for his incredible smile that seemed to never go away. As workers go, we had a winner.

But it got even better. Any chance Robert got, he told all the other guys about a God who could take a heroin-addled gang-banger, a loser who showed no mercy to the people he oppressed, and shower him with love and mercy in amounts he could have never dreamed.

His coworkers and other guys on the job sites started coming to Christ, lives were transformed, and I have to believe that entire families were, too. No one could look at and listen to Robert and not feel like they had been hit by a tidal wave of love. He even went to the streets where his cousins ran, and brought guys out of the gang life. In Robert, the Gospel came alive.

We liked Robert so much that when he, his wife and two kids needed somewhere to live, Karen and I offered to let them stay in our home. We wondered how it was going to go with eight people living together, but it was great. Karen and Robert's wife really hit it off, and so did their kids with ours. That period of time was a blessing to all of us.

> I wasn't sure what it was, but I knew it didn't look good.

One day, Robert showed up for work looking a bit different—at the very least, there was something about him I hadn't noticed before. He had large purple splotches underneath his skin and protruding bumps that appeared to be tumors. I wasn't sure what it was, but I knew it didn't look good. Later, he confided in me that he had contracted AIDS from sharing needles during his gang days. It was in the late 80s, and the only thing any of us knew about AIDS was that it was a death sentence. If you had it, you died. Period.

I looked at Robert's beautiful wife and kids. He had come so far and made such a difference in so many people's lives, introducing them to their eternity with Jesus. It was absolutely heartbreaking that it would all end so quickly. And yet, Robert's smile would not leave his face. Amazingly, Robert, instead of wondering *Why me*, thought, *Who else can I tell about Jesus while I still have time?*

At that time, Karen and I had started attending Yorba Linda Friends Church. It had experienced some upheaval, and in the process, the congregation dwindled down to around 200 people. John Werhas, a former Dodger, was the new pastor, and in trying to rebuild the church, saw that there was a gender imbalance among the leadership. It seemed as though the men had abdicated their roles, and women ran nearly everything at the church.

So, he called together a group of about seven men from the church to meet on Thursday mornings where the goal was to build them up to be leaders of their households, and then ultimately, the church.

I joined the group sometime after it began and found that I was the only non-white-collar worker there. All the men were traditional suit-and-tie-guys climbing up their respective corporate ladders. I wasn't in construction clothes, but it was easy to tell that one of us did not look like the others.

> I felt a need to dig deeper. I just didn't know how that was going to happen.

The group was great and I enjoyed meeting everyone. But for me, coming from the life-altering experience of MNBS where everybody got really real about their walk with Christ, this experience seemed to sit on the surface far too much. I felt a need to dig deeper. I just didn't know how that was going to happen.

Then it hit me. We rotated different people to lead the study each week, and when my turn came up, I thought, *Wouldn't it be great to invite Robert to speak? With all these stiff-collared guys, wouldn't Robert, with his gangbanger appearance and enthusiasm for Christ, blow them away?* I checked with John Werhas, and he was like, "Let's do it."

The day I showed up for the study with Robert at my side, I was feeling a little uneasy. *What would God do with this moment? Would the guys be a little repelled by Robert? Would they just shut down?*

I introduced Robert to the group, which had grown to about 17, and with his cholo vibe, intimidating tattoos, cropped hair, purple lesions, and protruding tumors, he stood, smiled broadly and spoke. He talked about drugs, gang and street life, hate and self-destruction in a way that, I'm willing to bet, none of the guys thought was possible outside of the movies. But he also spoke about the saving grace of Jesus, joy, love, and his excitement for each new day. All seventeen of them sat there with their eyes peeled as if blown open by a stiff wind. They were not just listening to a guy talking, they were watching a walking, living embodiment of the miracle of Christ's blood reviving a man's soul to life. They didn't know what hit them.

A rather quiet, real estate agent named Wes Brown was there that morning, someone who usually sat alone and kept to himself, began to have a physical reaction to what he was hearing. It was the beginning of a journey that, over a period of weeks, ultimately led him to a place of brokenness and desperation for everything Robert had.

In the moment that Wes Brown asked Jesus into his heart, he was also suddenly a man on a mission. He led his wife to Christ, and then started bringing people to Yorba Linda Friends Church by the droves. Friends, family, even clients were coming to know Christ through Wes. He soon left his job and took a leadership role in the men's ministry at the church. The ministry expanded exponentially. It was sweeping guys out of the neighborhoods and into the church in great waves with activities, outings, golf tournaments and more. The regular attendance numbers at Yorba Linda Friends jumped to 2,000. The number of lives changed by Wes' actions is, I am willing to bet, incalculable.

It was a golden period in my life, to witness all that God had done through the lives of unsuspecting players like Floyd Thorne, Mike and John Werhas, and a wayward son who stumbled onto a beach in Cabo San Lucas with a face full of tears.

Because, through all those lives, the morning of that Bible study was really a passing of the torch, a handing off, as it were, from Robert to Wes. None of us could have ever seen it coming. That's what makes it all the more amazing.

Wes is still touching lives for Christ today. And Robert, as he breathed his last breath, knew that he was able to live his final days with integrity and love. He knew that his son and daughter got to see their dad work hard and live for Jesus, and that he was going to be welcomed into the arms of his heavenly Father, who eagerly awaited him on just the other side of his momentarily dimmed smile.

Robert Mejia was a good and faithful servant if ever there was one.

FOR REFLECTION

When we took our focus off the success of the business and relinquished it into God's hands for His discretion, He expanded our influence, and thus, His influence in this world. By connecting MBW with Teen Challenge, it led to Robert and then to Wes, which led to changed lives in the barrios of Santa Ana as well as the affluent neighborhoods of Yorba Linda. God wants to use you to be a part of His plan to change lives. Are you willing? What are you holding onto that you can you offer God today so that your journey to greater influence can begin? Have you given Him your entire life—money, business, spouse…everything? How would your life change if you truly gave Him everything?

5

The Hand Off, Part II

THE MORNING THAT I TOOK ROBERT TO THE MEN'S BIBLE STUDY might have looked like a regular early-morning gathering of church-going men, but I think that was the morning God was playing chess in our midst. And, He had just made a killer move.

Wes Brown, the standoffish guy in the corner, who was there to fulfill a condition made by the woman he wanted to marry, began to sweat. And he didn't stop until his clothes were literally drenched through.

As Wes was leaving the Bible study, John Werhas noticed him, dressed in a three-piece suit and looking like he had just stepped out of a rainstorm. He was sopping wet. "Are you alright?" John asked. It caught the attention of all of us standing there. Suddenly we were concerned that Wes was having a heart attack. "I'm fine," he said, like he was coming apart. "I just need to get going."

Wes went home, shaken to the core by what he had just seen: A guy who was *dying* saying that he had absolutely no fear, but instead was filled with love and excitement. Wes, himself a former street gang member who hated all Mexican gangs, looked at Robert with irritation when he saw him walk in the room—latent hate from the past. There was no reason that Robert's story should have moved Wes or caused him to feel on the verge of an emotional meltdown. Besides, Wes had been an atheist ever since his beloved mother died. And, he was in no way passive about his beliefs. In his mind, there was no God. The concept was impossible. Ridiculous. Only idiots believe such a thing.

And yet his heart felt beaten up.

A few days later, we got word that Robert had been hospitalized and was spiraling downhill fast. It hit Wes hard. He was dumbfounded that Robert had been so close to death and still made the trip to the Bible study that morning to talk to a bunch of guys he didn't even know. *He could've died on the ride over to speak to us*, he thought. It drove him crazy. He couldn't think. He couldn't work. He called John Werhas and told him that he wanted to see Robert in the hospital. John suggested that perhaps all of the guys from the Bible study should go.

As we arrived at the hospital, it was clear that Wes had a lot on his mind—he had the furrowed brow of a man looking for answers. We entered Robert's hospital room to see Robert lying withered and small on his bed. He wore the color of a man on his last stretch of life. At such times, no one knows what to say, so we mostly just didn't. John spoke a few words of encouragement, and we all did our best to lend our voices to the sentiments John was offering. I'm sure Robert appreciated it. He just didn't need it. Robert, having refused all pain meds because he was, "done with drugs," began to testify to the love of Jesus. And then, with each man deeply moved and broken, Robert opened his mouth and began to sing weak songs of mighty praise. There wasn't a dry eye in the room. All any of us could muster was the sound of our sniffling noses. As Robert sang, he swallowed and grimaced hard under the excruciating pain as his body continued to break down inch by inch before our eyes. Even so, Robert, at times, smiled that smile.

As he continued to talk, he told us that after his 10-12 hour shifts for MBW, he went out into the streets to tell the drug dealers and the prostitutes about Jesus. He even brought them home to minister to them, and tried to get them back on their feet. Even with his body shutting down, he didn't want to be in the comforting arms of his wife. He felt he belonged among the painful lives out on the streets.

Wes recalls the feeling that nothing made sense. Right before his eyes, a man was passing away—and becoming new—at the same moment. Wes, who up to that point, lived life by his own strength, left the hospital feeling like his world had been flipped upside down. He now sensed that *everything worth living for* was something he knew nothing about.

A few days later, we received word that Robert died. We knew it was coming, and yet it still hit hard. Karen and I went to church that Sunday with heavy hearts. We missed our friend.

Wes sat in the pew with a particularly disgruntled expression on his face. John noticed—which I believe was Wes' hope. When the service was over, John came off the stage to talk to Wes and find out what his angst was all about.

"Robert died," Wes said.

"Yes, he did," John replied.

"Listen. You're not going to try to tell me everybody here in this church is saved and going to heaven, are you?" Wes asked.

"No."

"Well, then why didn't you ever put Robert up at that pulpit?"

"Do you believe everybody would have been saved if I had?" John asked.

"Yes," said Wes. "With every fiber in my body."

John looked at him. "What about you? Did Robert affect you that way?"

Wes gave John a stern look. "Don't go there. Don't put that on me. I'm asking you if God is a loving God, and He wanted all these people to know Him, why did Robert have to die and why didn't he ever get your pulpit?"

"How do you know," John asked, "that God didn't take Robert Mejia home after meeting you, just so you could become a believer?"

It sent a charge through Wes' body. "You're saying that God traded Robert's life, this young man with a wife and kids, for mine? You don't want to go there. If I continue on with this conversation, I'm going to say things that I don't think you want me to say."

"You and I are having lunch tomorrow," John said as if it was a fact.

"I'm not having lunch with you. I know what you're going to try to do, and better men than you have tried to convince me of God and they never got close, so forget it."

"Are you having lunch with me or not?"

"OK, let's put it this way. I will have lunch with you, but know this. The gloves are coming off. You're going to get everything I have because I don't believe any of this garbage."

"Lunch at 12?" John asked.

The next day, John gave Wes an earful of the Gospel. Wes batted everything back for nearly two hours. When John felt like all his points had been made, he said, "So, are you ready?"

"Ready for what?"

"To receive Jesus Christ as your Lord and Savior?"

Wes laughed. "Receive Jesus Christ? That's the best you got? You think you got me after that? Look," Wes said, placing the saltshaker in the middle of the table, "you know God, right?

NOT MY BUSINESS

You ask God to move this saltshaker just one inch *right now* and I will give Him my life until the day I die."

"How dare you," John said coldly. "You want me to ask God to do some cheap trick to prove to you He exists when everybody who believed before you came by faith? You're actually asking God for a magic show?"

Wes didn't reply.

"You're not worth it," John said with surprising curtness.

Wes' temperature suddenly rose. He wasn't expecting that.

"I wouldn't ask God to do that, even if I could. You better think about that." John gave a stern look. "Are you a betting man, Wes?"

"If I think I can win."

"Well then," John said, "let me ask you something. What have you lost if the Bible is untrue?"

"Nothing, I guess."

"And, what have you lost if the Bible is true?"

Wes gulped. He knew the answer was everything. And he knew that his life, with that bet on the table, amounted to nothing. Most of all, he knew that if he accepted Christ, he would gain everything his heart ever wanted. Without Him, life wasn't worth living.

John said, "I don't like that bet. How 'bout you?"

Wes had to get out of there. Later, at home, he offered an "I-might-as-well" invitation for Christ to come into his heart, but knew deep inside it was more like circling the airport than landing.

The memorial service for Robert was held the following weekend in a little chapel in Santa Ana. Karen and I arrived to see guys from work, along with Wes, and a section of menacing-looking Mexican guys sitting together, headbands on and sunglasses drawn—as if they were ready to rumble. "This should be interesting," I thought. "If we all get out of here alive."

As friends and family stood to eulogize Robert, a large gang-banger stood and got in line to speak. All eyes went to him and the tension rose. As he stepped up and took the microphone, his homeys erupted. "Yeah, tell 'em, man!" they yelled, clapping hands and whooping it up. The whole chapel seemed to go on high alert. The banger turned around and stared down the audience. The place went cold. "Robert Mejia killed my brother in a drug deal," he said in a thick, intimidating accent. Everyone did a collective gulp. "When he got out of prison, I heard he was standing on a crate in the park—preaching. So, I walked up to Robert and there was a crowd listening to him. I decided to wait until he was finished so that way when I pulled out my piece and blew him away, everybody would see that his God couldn't protect him from me. So I waited, and I listened." Every person in that chapel went silent. "And when he was finished," he said as everybody braced themselves, "I gave my life to Jesus Christ. And I forgave Robert."

The section of gangbangers erupted again, cheering and clapping. They were all believers—another testimony to the faithfulness of Robert Mejia.

Wes broke down right then and there and cried like a baby. He didn't understand it, but he knew he wanted it. The power of forgiveness was undeniable. Wes was now all in. I wonder if he had any inkling of what was about to happen in and through him—the kind of impact he would have.

But of course, he didn't. That's the beauty of a life lived with Jesus. When I thought MBW was nothing more than just a way of making a living, it turned out that when we added Robert to the payroll, the company became a pivotal player in thousands of changed lives.

FOR REFLECTION

When you look at the purpose of your life, how big is your vision? Have you considered the "ripple" your impact can make in the ocean of life? Is God using you to affect lives and generations beyond you? In what ways can you become more proactive in becoming part of God's story to reach others? Do you believe it is something you can start by taking control or by relinquishing? Is it a scheduling issue, or a heart issue?

Think back on when you first accepted Christ into your heart. Do you think it came about because of others who had relinquished their lives to God so that He could use them to reach others?

6

Being Bill

POOR TOM STANLEY. The eighth-grader had no idea when he walked into my class at St. Barbara Catholic School that I, a seventh-grader, suddenly had designs on his time. Our basketball team didn't have a center. Tom was thin, gangly and uncoordinated, but at 5'11", he was the tallest kid in the class. That meant he was going to play center on our basketball team whether he wanted to or not. I wanted to win.

Elgin Baylor, Jerry West, Gail Goodrich, Wilt Chamberlain, Happy Hairston, Keith Erickson and Jim McMillan were the players that made up the top tier of the Los Angeles Lakers in the late 60s and early 70s. When coach Bill Sharman put five of them on the court, they moved as one. Through much of my childhood, they racked up remarkably exciting wins and amazing seasons, dominated the West, and in 1972, they won 33 games in a row. They had an unthinkable win-loss record of 69-

13, and took the NBA Championship in just five games over the Knicks. It was an incredibly exciting time. Their amazing focus and drive toward excellence was not lost on me. Anyone could see that Bill Sharman had whipped those players into a finely tuned machine. I was going to do that with my middle school basketball team—I was going to be Bill. That's right. I was twelve.

"Hey Tom," I said to him with a snap of my head when we walked out of class for lunch, "over here." I didn't even ask him if he wanted to play basketball. I just knew that all my classmates, while good basketball players, were shrimps. If we were going to dominate, we needed to be a well-rounded team, and in order to do that, we had to have a center who could hold his own. Tom was going to be it. The best thing about him was his good attitude. He was willing to work and follow my instructions to a T.

And so, I drilled Tom relentlessly on how to rebound, how to sell a fake, how to block a shot, how to shoot a hook, and how to post up. "Again! Do it again!" I would yell. I did everything but blow a whistle and make him hit the showers.

Years later, when my kids were playing sports, I remember seeing parents with hotshot kids, looking for other hotshot kids and their parents to band together and form a team where all the talent was centralized in their sons. With at least two dominant players, they believed they could overpower the other teams. But, this was almost always a mistake. If a mediocre group of guys played as a *team* and evenly distributed the talent—as long as they operated efficiently and intelligently—they regularly took down the talent-rich team.

That's what I focused on when I coached my kids' teams. I knew my team could beat those talent-heavy teams if I drilled them on the fundamentals and playmaking, instead of just shooting. And whenever I got a kid who really struggled, I worked with him on those fundamentals. I knew that we were only as good as our weakest player. If I raised his game, I raised our whole team.

> First, I had to lead by example. Second, I had to demand a lot.

Years later when I was building my business at MBW and creating teams for caulking jobs in town, I looked around at the faces before me and it wasn't particularly encouraging. The guys available to choose from, cocaine addicts, potheads, or alcoholics, were not exactly the choirboys of caulking. In fact, one of them used to regale us with stories of how he used to knock off liquor stores. I'm not talking high character individuals here.

And yet, I knew I had to turn them into Mini Me's because I was entrusting them with my reputation. There were two ways that this was going to happen. First, I had to lead by example. Second, I had to demand a lot. The reason I saw my task in this specific order was because before I could ever demand a lot, I had to show them that everything I told them to do, I was willing to do myself. When I told them to move up and down the ladders with urgency, they had to see that's how I did it. When I told them to keep their clothes clean, they had to see me looking good. You get the picture.

And so, after I exemplified what I wanted, I laid a heck of a list on them: Don't show up late. Don't let your site area have any trash. Don't waste materials. Don't let your pace slow. Don't get material on your clothes. Don't ask when you are done (the answer will always be *when we're finished*). Don't complain to anybody. Don't chew the fat while working. Don't go on breaks unless we all do. Don't let me catch you walking when you should be running.

Or, if the positive is preferred, be early to work. Be tidy. Be mindful of the cost of the material. Move with efficiency in mind. Be clean so you can keep the trucks and equipment clean. Trust me that I will not forget to tell you when you can knock off. Keep any negative comments to yourself. Concentrate on your work—talking only slows the pace. Take breaks as a team—individuals taking breaks lowers the efficiency of the team. If you find the team is waiting for you, run!

> If you find the team is waiting for you, run!

I know it is a lot to keep in mind, but the success of the team required it. And, it is hard to quarrel with the result. We started growing, and suddenly, we had many subcontractors calling MBW to do their jobs. I had to expand fast in order to handle the work, which created the good problem of how to have the company broaden while keeping the teams running efficiently.

So, as a measure of quality control, I put the focus on "screening" new hires, which was a way of weeding out the good from the bad *as I trained them*. If they sauntered rather than ran, they were gone. If they rolled their eyes at my instructions, they were gone. If they felt they didn't need to fill the gun the way I told them, they were gone. If they left trash in their area, they were gone. If they wasted material, well…you get it.

They had to buy into the process in every way. You can teach a person to perform a task, but it's much harder and time-consuming to teach them to have an open mind to someone's seemingly ridiculous demands. This wasn't so much a job as it was *a role on a team*. The thinking had to be corporate rather than individual.

Yes, I did fire a lot of guys right off the bat. They were bouncing off our payroll list like a Wilt Chamberlain free throw. For every 10 guys who answered our *help wanted ads*, I probably kept three. But that's how we became the best, fastest, most reliable caulking company on the West coast. I just couldn't keep a guy who thought he knew better than me on how to caulk a building. The team's efficiency needed to be protected and enhanced at all times. The team was sacrosanct.

As we grew, I found that I simply didn't have the time to teach everybody how to be a Mini-Me. I had to get my leads, my top employees, to teach the new hires to be what I needed. The problem was that the leads were so ingrained with the idea of being productive, that they had a hard time letting their productivity decline to take the time to teach. I was cool with less productivity as long as they were bringing up the new guys to be incredible team players. I knew the productivity would be there again, and if the new hires worked out well and caught on to the concept, all the better. For me, it was a good example of how much buy-in my leads actually experienced, how much heart-change had actually occurred—even if it did cause a problem in getting them to *teach speed to the detriment of their own pace.*

But I guess that's the crux of it all. I didn't just create guys who could merely do a task. I created workers who bought into an idea that hard work was its own reward because to work amazingly, was to feel amazing. To work efficiently makes people happy—the boss, the client and the worker himself. To be neat and clean makes the worker stand up taller with pride. To refrain from wasting material gives the worker a sense that his work is valuable. It's not just a paycheck. It's a way of giving oneself a greater sense of meaning.

And so, without really even noticing, I had stepped into Ron Reed's shoes. I had completely embraced his *work-is-art* approach. How a person worked was a reflection of how he felt about himself, and vice versa.

The process allowed me to put a team of five outstanding workers on the job to work as one, and to move in unison with the objective of making our clients incredibly happy. We did it by being efficient, clean, fast and good. And we started dominating the West. I loved the feeling. I loved winning.

I was finally Bill Sharman.

FOR REFLECTION

Ephesians 6:5-7 (NIV) says, "Slaves, obey your earthly masters with respect and fear, and with sincerity of heart, just as you would obey Christ. Obey them not only to win their favor when their eye is on you, but as slaves of Christ, doing the will of God from your heart. Serve wholeheartedly, as if you were serving the Lord, not people…."

What is your personal work ethic? Even if you are a supervisor or business owner, are you working as if unto God? How can you ask others for 100% if they don't see it in you? What is on the line, besides productivity, if others witness your lack-luster performance? Is your work a job, a ministry, or a testimony?

Focus on your work today and bring it before the Lord. Ask Him to fill you with a new perspective on your work's potential to serve and glorify Him, and to reach others for His sake.

7

My Answer

"YOU HAD A QUESTION?" I asked the young woman in the third row with her hand raised.

"Hi, Mr. Beamish" she said, rather professionally. "Were you able to establish a screening-to-hire ratio?"

"Well, no, not really," I replied. "I don't really know the ratio." Another hand went up from a young male student in the back. "Yes?" I asked.

"Considering your rather strident screening process," he said, "how did your company reduce the cost of hiring new employees, and what exactly is the difference between the cost of hiring and the cost of firing? I'd also like to know how both affect the bottom line."

NOT MY BUSINESS

It was probably the ninth question from business students at Vanguard University, a Christian College in Southern California. I was speaking to them as a favor to my friend Ed Westbrook, a professor at the University. My entire speech that day was to convey just how unconventional my business journey was, particularly given that the only business book I ever read was the Holy Bible, and how its principles taught me, changed me, sent me on a path toward building a multimillion-dollar company, and helped me maintain it.

Apparently, I wasn't getting my point across.

The eager students with future business prospects simply didn't have a lens for this kind of rhetoric. They needed charts, graphs, ratios and percentages. It was as though I walked into a French class and spoke to them in Japanese. *It just wasn't computing.*

As I stood there feeling more and more helpless with each question, I looked into those young faces staring back at me. They appeared to be light years away from understanding my story and message. They weren't that much older than me when I was a student on a high school trip in Paris in 1971. That's when I got a letter from my friend Donnie Kobayashi saying how sorry he was to hear the news.

"What news?"

My dad had died of cancer, and the news had spread around before my mom decided to tell me. Perhaps she didn't want to ruin my trip, knowing that I would be home soon anyway. Nevertheless, it was awful.

My relationship with my dad was a little empty to begin with as he was mostly gone from the house, working and doing whatever he was doing. His sudden, permanent departure left me feeling even more incomplete. That's why the things that I had grown up to believe were important, suddenly weren't anymore. Like school. What was the point?

So, along with my brothers, John and Paul, we would get up in the morning and load our surfboards into our early 60s, blue, Ford Fairlane, and head on down to Huntington Beach to surf, knowing that we'd get to school when we darn well felt like it. Because in the water, sliding down the front of the waves off the north side of the pier felt exciting. Most of life didn't present anything like that. My hair was long, my body was tanned and I knew I looked good. The blonde beach babes with their long hair and tanned bodies looked good, too, and for a young guy hoping for a little respite from a painful life, it was the perfect arrangement. And so, regrettably, I took advantage of it.

And, of course, my head and thoughts were steeped in a cloud of pot smoke at nearly all times. Surfing, girls, and pot—they were three highs that I almost never came back from. I think back on that period and see how close I was to sinking into that life forever—living on the beach and submerged in the *I don't care lifestyle*. I had seen older dudes who had lived it; salty guys who knew their way around a wave and a waitress, but couldn't do life. I'd see them under the pier, sleeping off a drunken stupor or a pot-induced high. Invariably, their hair would be long and grey, their skin would be beaten down by the sun, voices rough, eyes a touch sad, vocabularies filled with *man* and *dude* as a badge of honor to say they never gave in to society, and their heads would be filled with the fantasy of being Robert August from The Endless Summer. These were guys who had stepped off the sidewalk of life one day, and it felt so good out there on the sand that they simply never got back on. I knew their world. I was from their world. Like me, they just wanted to feel good.

So, that's where I was headed; toward a life in the shadows of the Huntington Beach pier where I would probably spend my days chasing down another wave, another hit, and another conquest. And, I would probably spend my nights lying in a beat up car with a surfboard laying across the seats, nursing broken dreams and a couple of sexually transmitted diseases, smoking pot and falling asleep listening to the Dodgers, while fantasizing that I was Sandy Koufax or Robert August.

But God had other plans. When I accepted Jesus into my heart, it took hold of me like nothing else. I couldn't believe God would do so much to claim me for Himself as if He just had to have me. When I started to attend Monday Night Bible Study, which grew to be 300 teenagers strong, I entered into that environment at a remarkable moment in time. There I was, suddenly with a bunch of guys who were just like me, sharing my life and struggles to a T: difficult and painful family lives, drug pasts, blue collar dads who were emotionally detached, and a bit of Catholic disillusionment. When we began reading the Bible together, we couldn't believe it as the words came to life and seemed to jump off the pages like a pop-up book. Our excitement fed off each other, and the wave of joy we rode was thrilling. A couple of guys who had grown up in the church joined us, but they couldn't manage to find the joy we had.

Coming from their intact families and Christian upbringings, it was hard for them to see the light in their well-lit lives. As for me, *I knew what I had been saved from.*

And while I was thrilled to know there was a God who loved me, I think part of the reason I read the Bible so voraciously was because once I realized that God is a personal God, I really wanted to know what He wanted *me* to know. I think I was looking for a father figure to tell me what to do. That's what happens when something deep inside tells you that you really aren't a whole person. And so, I read my Bible like a lost boy looking for a secret message from his dad. I was excited beyond belief to read about how much God loved me, but it wasn't until I came upon a book called Proverbs that I nearly fell off my chair. There it was: Instruction.

The practical nature of Proverbs blew my mind and ignited my heart. My dad never taught me how to do so many of the things in life that I would have looked to him for, and now he never would. Suddenly, from the quill of Solomon, King David's own son, came guidance for how to work, how to live, how to spend money, how to marry…I couldn't believe it. *You mean I don't have to figure out life all on my own?*

The best thing about Proverbs was that it wasn't just telling me what to do, it was trying to tell me how to be, how to think, what principles to build life on—all for my own success and joy! The possibilities almost seemed too much to fathom. Here I was, a dumb kid right off the beach looking into a sea of wisdom. Was I really about to become…wise? Me?

As I began to read Proverbs, the words and concepts began to jump out at me. They were all the things I wanted for my life. Things like:

How to have integrity (2:6-9)

How to gain favor and good repute in God's sight and among men (3:3-4)

How to work (10:2-5)

Why you should be slow to speak (17:27-28)

What not to love (21:17)

Why you should maintain a good name (22:1)

The importance of humility (22:4)

What being generous will bring you (22:9)

Why you should pay a fair wage (22:16)

I couldn't believe what I was reading. The more I looked, the more I saw my path, like a cobblestone road being laid out before me as I walked. And so, I eagerly followed. One of the first things that happened was that I kept finding myself in the company of a girl by the name of Karen. She attended MNBS and had grown up in the Friend's Church where the Bible study met. Unlike the beach blondes that I had been dating, she was Spanish with lovely dark hair, olive skin, and green eyes. She was beautiful. I was smitten immediately. As we began to date, I discovered her great sense of humor and that her highest calling was to have children and raise them to know and love God. When she talked about her faith, that's when I felt like Ol' King Solomon started nodding his head, saying, *Yes, my son, a woman like her*. The more she revealed her feelings about God, the more I felt myself falling deeper in love. At one of her school banquets, I even saw her get up and speak boldly about Jesus and the importance of trusting in God. She was giving her friends the keys to life at the risk of being judged and rejected. I was so impressed. What a loving person she was, and still is.

Even though I was in love with Karen, after about a year of dating we found a reason to break up, as many young couples do. It wasn't long after our break-up that I met another great-looking girl who was just like the ones I used to date. She had a long mane, a risqué style, and an I-know-I'm-hot personality. When we started dating, I remember getting looks from my friends that seemed to say, *Yes, that's the Mark we know and love. That's the kind of girl you should be dating.* But it wasn't a case of the more I got to know her, the less I liked her. Surprisingly, the more I got to know her, the more I missed Karen. As I read Proverbs and learned the anatomy of wisdom, it became clear that Karen was a part of my future. Nothing else felt right. King Solomon had spoken mightily in my life again. Karen and I were married on Valentine's Day in 1976.

That's why when it came time for running a business, I felt no need to read a textbook, find a consultant, or take a class. I just keep doing what I had been doing—reading the Bible, Proverbs in particular, with Karen at my side. She was my partner in every way, doing the company's books, taking calls and ordering materials, all while keeping house and raising our two sons. We worked hard, prayed, entrusted every aspect to God, believed that He would prosper us—as long as money was never our goal—and took King Solomon's words to heart. And sure enough, MBW grew bigger than I could have ever dreamed.

In 1981, we were running MBW out of our garage. By 2005, we were doing jobs all over California , Arizona, Nevada, Colorado, Oklahoma, New York, Washington, Kentucky, Hawaii, Oregon, New Mexico, and Mexico, and billing more than 15 million dollars a year. MBW's accounts included Universal Studios, San Diego Zoo, University of Southern California, and Dodger Stadium at Chavez Ravine. I even got to be the chaplain for the Dodgers, becoming friendly with many of the players as well as Tommy Lasorda and his wife, Jo—all this from a kid who didn't have a clue what he was going to do with his life, didn't finish college and preferred to play his days away. That's how I know all this success has nothing to do with me. My only part was a willingness to submit, where maybe others wouldn't. If I have to come down somewhere, maybe that is it.

"Mr. Beamish, how were you able to maintain profitability after the economic slowdown?" the next student asked.

The Word of God, dude, I should have said. *My success is entirely about God and not about anything I did. Can you handle that?*

So, let's review. I was a father-starved, pot-smoking, girl-chasing, uneducated young man with no ambition who God ultimately gave a multi-million dollar business that provided a great standard of living for hundreds of people, and enabled me to contribute millions of dollars to Kingdom-building endeavors. Who could do that but God? And if that isn't enough proof that He had stepped into my life in a mighty way, get this. When I was the chaplain of the Dodgers, I was able to stand on a baseball field in Vero Beach, Florida and chat with Sandy Koufax—*the* Sandy Koufax—the guy in my radio and fantasies as a kid. What an extraordinary thrill. When I go down and surf near my second home in Costa Rica, that's a story my surf buddy Robert August loves to hear.

Any other questions?

> **MARK'S FAVORITE PROVERBS**
>
> 1:7 (NIV) "The fear of the LORD is the beginning of knowledge, but fools despise wisdom and instruction."
>
> 2:6-8 (NIV) "For the Lord gives wisdom; from his mouth come knowledge and understanding. He holds success in store for the upright, he is a shield to those whose walk is blameless, for he guards the course of the just and protects the way of his faithful ones."
>
> 3:3-4 (NIV) "Let love and faithfulness never leave you; bind them around your neck, write them on the tablet of your heart. Then you will win favor and a good name in the sight of God and man."
>
> 3:9-10 (NIV) "Honor the Lord with your wealth, with the firstfruits of all your crops; then your barns will be filled to overflowing, and your vats will brim over with new wine."

8:10-21 (NASB) "Take my instruction and not silver, and knowledge rather than choicest gold. "For wisdom is better than jewels, and all desirable things cannot compare with her. "I, wisdom, dwell with prudence, and I find knowledge and discretion.

"The fear of the Lord is to hate evil; Pride and arrogance and the evil way

And the perverted mouth, I hate."Counsel is mine and sound wisdom; I am understanding, power is mine."By me, kings reign, and rulers decree justice.

"By me princes rule, and nobles, All who judge rightly."I love those who love me; And those who diligently seek me will find me."Riches and honor are with me, Enduring wealth and righteousness."My fruit is better than gold, even pure gold, and my yield better than choicest silver. "I walk in the way of righteousness, In the midst of the paths of justice, To endow those who love me with wealth, that I may fill their treasuries.

10:2-5 (NASB) Ill-gotten gains do not profit, But righteousness delivers from death. The Lord will not allow the righteous to hunger, But He will reject the craving of the wicked. Poor is he who works with a negligent hand, But the hand of the diligent makes rich. He who gathers in summer is a son who acts wisely, but he who sleeps in harvest is a son who acts shamefully.

13:11 (NASB) Wealth obtained by fraud dwindles, but the one who gathers by labor increases it.

14:23 (NASB) In all labor there is profit, but mere talk leads only to poverty.

17:27-28 (NASB) He who restrains his words has knowledge, and he who has a cool spirit is a man of understanding. Even a fool, when he keeps silent, is considered wise; When he closes his lips, he is considered prudent.

20:4 (NASB) The sluggard does not plow after the autumn, So he begs during the harvest and has nothing.

21:17 (NASB) He who loves pleasure will become a poor man; He who loves wine and oil will not become rich.

21:25-27 (NASB) "The desire of the sluggard puts him to death, For his hands refuse to work; All day long he is craving, While the righteous gives and does not hold back. The sacrifice of the wicked is an abomination. . . ."

22:1 (NASB) "A good name is to be more desired than great wealth, Favor is better than silver and gold."

22:4 (NASB) "The reward of humility and the fear of the Lord, Are riches, honor, and life."

22:9 (NASB) "He who is generous will be blessed, For he gives some of his food to the poor."

22:16 (NASB) "He who oppresses the poor to make

more for himself, Or who gives to the rich, will only come to poverty."

22:29 (NIV) "Do you see someone skilled in their work? They will serve before kings; they will not serve before officials of low rank."

23:4 (NASB) "Do not weary yourself to gain wealth, Cease from your consideration of it."

24:27 (NASB) "Prepare your work outside, And make it ready for yourself in the field; Afterwards, then, build your house."

25:6-7 (NASB) "Do not claim honor in the presence of the king, And do not stand in the place of great men; For it is better that it be said to you, "Come up here," Than for you to be placed lower in the presence of the prince, Whom your eyes have seen."

27:2 (NASB) "Let another praise you, and not your own mouth; A stranger, and not your own lips."

27:18 (NASB) "He who tends the fig tree will eat its fruit, And he who cares for his master will be honored."

27:23-27 (NASB) "Know well the condition of your flocks, And pay attention to your herds; For riches are not forever, Nor does a crown endure to all generations. When the grass disappears, the new growth is seen, And the herbs of the mountains are gathered in, The lambs will be for your clothing, And the goats will bring the price of a field, And there will be goats' milk enough for your food, For the food of your household ...."

28:6 (NASB) "Better is the poor who walks in his integrity Than he who is crooked though he be rich."

29:20 (NASB) "Do you see a man who is hasty in his words? There is more hope for a fool than for him."

31:4-9 (NASB) "It is not for kings, O Lemuel, It is not for kings to drink wine, Or for rulers to desire strong drink, For they will drink and forget what is decreed, And pervert the rights of all the afflicted. Give strong drink to him who is perishing, And wine to him whose life is bitter. Let him drink and forget his poverty And remember his trouble no more. Open your mouth for the mute, For the rights of all the unfortunate. Open your mouth, judge righteously, And defend the rights of the afflicted and needy."

FOR REFLECTION

Faith in Jesus Christ as your sustenance for life requires an extreme approach, one that will likely go against cultural norms. Could it be that God is asking you for less reliance on conventional paths, i.e. how-to books, business mentoring, round tables, and is, instead, asking for reliance on His Word to direct your company and career? If you gave your business over to God completely, what would that look like?

Does that seem like folly? Would God say it was folly? If you were to utilize a mix of conventional business tools such as the ones listed above (books, mentoring, seminars, degrees) and God's Word, where do you believe God's Word should rank?

8

The Adrenaline Rush

IF THE BEAMISH HOUSEHOLD WAS CHAOTIC BEFORE 1971, and it was, it was nothing compared to what happened after my dad's death to cancer in the summer of that year. It was like a bomb had been detonated in our already tumultuous home at 9721 Oasis Street. Our family, including Mom, John, Paul, and our youngest brothers, Willie and David, ages 5 and 2, was in *free fall*. The sadness we all experienced at my dad's death was simply nothing Mom was equipped to handle—how could she? There were too many of us. The pain was too great. And she was perhaps most devastated of all. It left us bare to the world, just aching souls floundering about, looking for someone or something to stop the hurt.

When my mom received the life insurance check, she tried to do the smart thing. She gave it to a friend to invest, but the friend promptly lost it all. Suddenly, Mom, who was not really a stabilizing force to begin with, found herself spending large chunks of the day away from home as she was forced to take a job as a cafeteria worker for the school district. This left three high school boys at home to tend to our younger brothers and get good and ticked off about it. The fighting in the house was awful and constant, with despair, hopelessness and aimlessness stoking the flames. We were broke, alone and hurt, and we were profoundly angry at each other, at Mom, at life, at Dad. It didn't matter. Our house was a nest of hornets.

Mom moved with urgency at all times, as every segment of her day was another moment she had to get right, from getting the boys up, to getting to work, to getting home to make dinner, to cleaning the house, to running errands, to putting the young ones to bed. And, she did it all with a terrible case of heart sickness. Each day was like living through a fire drill.

I was the classic angry young man attracted to all the wrong things. The problem was all the wrong things felt so much better than what toeing the moral line had to offer. So I did them, then I felt guilty about doing them, which made me angry all over again. The aimlessness of it all, and the guilt-without-end cycle plays on your mind and body, and tells you you've already seen the trajectory of your life—and it's bleak. Dad was gone, Mom was emotionally gone, and, with all the pot I was smoking, so was I.

One day, when I actually decided to listen at school, career was the topic and, surprisingly, I took seriously the question they posed to us: What would I like to do with my life?

I went home and told my mom my crazy fantasy that being a sports announcer like Vin Scully would be a great career.

She never affirmed the idea, or said that maybe I should go to school to be a journalist, or that I should do this or that, nor did she make it sound like she took my future seriously enough to lend her concern. Maybe, there was another load of laundry to do, or a dinner to make, and that was the only thing on her mind. I don't know.

But for a time, it broke me. I had no encouragement, no direction, no plan, and it sure didn't seem like anyone cared about me, or my future.

Not long after, Alamitos Friends Church was sending their youth to a camp called Quaker Meadow, and my brother, Paul, was invited to go by a friend. When he got back, he walked in the house with a palpable peace about him that I hadn't seen before. Paul was a rather mellow guy anyway, but this was different. *Hmm.* I thought. *What's this all about?*

Later, when his new friends from camp came to the house, I noticed the whole lot of them had the same peaceful grin on their faces. They were all so calm and joyful. I wanted that. I was tired of being so angry.

A few months later, Paul invited some of his new friends over to watch his homemade surf movies, after which they watched a televised Billy Graham Crusade. So, I joined in. That's when I heard Billy say, "God has a plan for your life."

My life?

If God had a plan, tttll I needed to know—because a plan was exactly what I didn't have; it was exactly where the road ended for me. I got on my knees and asked Jesus into my heart.

Knowing I was saved and would never be alone filled me with joy and excitement, but He was just getting warmed up. Because, one night soon after, I opened the Bible and this spilled out:

> ## MATTHEW 6:25-34 (TLB)
>
> So my counsel is: Don't worry about things—food, drink, and clothes. For you already have life and a body—and they are far more important than what to eat and wear. Look at the birds! They don't worry about what to eat—they don't need to sow or reap or store up food—for your heavenly Father feeds them. And you are far more valuable to him than they are. Will all your worries add a single moment to your life?
>
> And why worry about your clothes? Look at the field lilies! They don't worry about theirs. Yet King Solomon in all his glory was not clothed as beautifully as they. And if God cares so wonderfully for flowers that are here today and gone tomorrow, won't he more surely care for you, O men of little faith?
>
> So don't worry at all about having enough food and clothing. Why be like the heathen? For they take pride in all these things and are deeply concerned about them. But your heavenly Father already knows perfectly well that you need them, and he will give them to you if you give him first place in your life and live as he wants you to.

TOP LEFT: MY DAD WITH HIS SISTER, MARGE, TOP RIGHT: DAD WITH HIS FAVORITE JACKET, BOTTOM LEFT: DAD'S BUSINESS HEADSHOT, BOTTOM RIGHT: DAD AT HOME

TOP LEFT: MOM AND DAD, TOP RIGHT: WILLIAM BILL BEAMISH COLLEGE PORTRAIT, BOTTOM LEFT: CHRISTMAS ON SANTA'S LAP, BOTTOM RIGHT: AS A TODDLER WITH HIS DAD

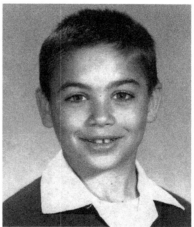

TOP: MARK WITH HIS FATHER, CENTER LEFT: MARK AS A BOY WITH HIS BROTHERS, CENTER RIGHT: GRADE SCHOOL, BOTTOM LEFT: SIX YEARS OLD, BOTTOM CENTER: BASEBALL DAYS, BOTTOM RIGHT: MIDDLE SCHOOL PORTRAIT

TOP: MARK, BROTHERS JOHN AND PAUL WITH MY DAD'S MOTHER, BERNICE, BOTTOM LEFT: PROM NIGHT, BOTTOM RIGHT: SENIOR PHOTO

TOP: WITH GRANDMA BERNICE RIGHT BEFORE DAD PASSED IN 1971, BOTTOM LEFT: TEENAGER AT HOME WITH HOTDOGS, BOTTOM RIGHT: TEENAGER

TOP LEFT: MARK AT HOME, TOP RIGHT: DATING KAREN, CENTER LEFT: DRESSED UP WITH KAREN 1975, CENTER RIGHT: AT PARK WITH KAREN AND PAUL, BOTTOM: HOME PLAYING POOL WITH KAREN

TOP LEFT: MARK AND KAREN TEENAGERS DATING, TOP RIGHT: WITH KAREN, CENTER LEFT: OUR WEDDING WITH PARENTS, CENTER RIGHT: ME, JOHN, PAUL WILLIE AND DAVID ON MOM'S LAP, BOTTOM: MARK, DONNIE, GARY AND BROTHER PAUL 1977

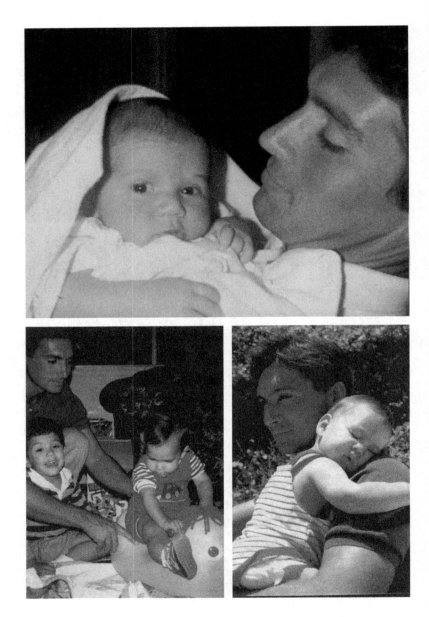

TOP: MARK WITH ADAM, FOUR WEEKS OLD. BOTTOM LEFT: BLAKE'S 1ST BIRTHDAY. BOTTOM RIGHT: HOLDING BLAKE AT DISNEYLAND

TOP LEFT: FEEDING BLAKE A BOTTLE, TOP RIGHT: MARK WITH THE BOYS, ADAM AND BLAKE, BOTTOM LEFT: MARK AND KAREN IN HAWAII, BOTTOM RIGHT: MARK WITH THE BOYS, ANAHEIM HOUSE

TOP LEFT: MARK WITH ADAM 4, BLAKE 2, TOP RIGHT: ORANGE COUNTY MARATHON, CENTER: ADAM POST ACCIDENT 1992, BOTTOM LEFT: MARK WITH THE BOYS AT DISNEYLAND, BOTTOM RIGHT: HALLOWEEN WITH THE BOYS

TOP: MARK WITH WALT AND PAT 1992, BOTTOM LEFT: UTAH 2/91 JUST BEFORE ADAM'S ACCIDENT, CENTER RIGHT: COACHING BASKETBALL, BOTTOM RIGHT: MARK AND BOYS AUG 1997

TOP: WITH EMPLOYEES ADAM 7TH GRADE, BOTTOM LEFT: BLAKE AND ADAM WITH DODGER BRETT BUTLER, BOTTOM RIGHT: MARK IN THE CO-PILOT SEAT

TOP: MARK'S FAMILY, BOTTOM: MBW CREW

TOP LEFT: FIRST SURF TRIP TO COSTA RICA WITH EMPLOYEES JIM GRIFFITHS AND BERTO SAHAGUN, TOP RIGHT: PLAYA NEGRA '05, CENTER LEFT: SURFER MARK, CENTER RIGHT: CHRISTMAS 2000, BOTTOM: MBW SALES REWARD TRIP TO MAUI

TOP: WITH ELDERS YORBA LINDA FRIENDS CHURCH 2001, CENTER LEFT: MBW EMPLOYEES AT A GOLF TOURNAMENT, CENTER RIGHT: MARK AND KAREN IN ITALY, BOTTOM LEFT: MARK AND BOYS FATHERS DAY 2014, BOTTOM RIGHT: MARK AND ADAM ENJOY RUNNING TOGETHER

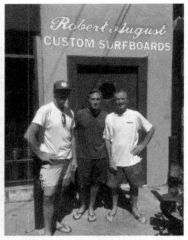

TOP LEFT: MARK GOLFING, TOP RIGHT: MARK WITH ROBERT AUGUST AND SAM AUGUST, CENTER LEFT: MODERN LUXURY ORANGE COUNTY DIGITAL EDITION, CENTER RIGHT: MARK AND FLOYD THORNE AT CAMP, BOTTOM: MARK AT HOME WITH FLOYD

> So don't be anxious about tomorrow. God will take care of your tomorrow too. Live one day at a time.
>
> And from Proverbs 3:5-6 (NLT)
>
> "Trust in the lord with all your heart; do not depend on your own understanding. Seek his will in all you do, and he will show you which path to take."

That's when I did something very unlike me; I bought it. I consumed those words, each one, hook, line, and sinker. I was like, *Done. I'm in.*

But, before I make it sound like it was a decision, it wasn't. The way I bought-in was similar to the way a baby buys into language; as if it was being imprinted on my soul. When Jesus said, essentially, *I'm in control of what happens to you, and now you are free to live and pursue what you want in Christ—just trust Me*—somewhere deep inside, I was stamped with it. Freedom now ran through my veins.

Truthfully, it was a lot like my other addictions, surfing, girls and pot, with one exception. Jesus in my heart felt better than all of them put together.

When I finally split from Sam in 1986, I led MBW with the full conviction that God meant what He said about having my back. And so, I just did it. I went forward happily, and rather obliviously. Imagine that. Everywhere I stepped, I did so without the fear that I might be making a wrong move. The way I saw it, God was the one who had filled me with hope and joy

NOT MY BUSINESS

and had forgiven all my sins. He was also the one who said, "Don't worry about it. I work everything in your life for good." To me, that was not meant as a suggestion.

Early on, when I was just getting started with my business, I stored material for our jobs along the side of my house. When we ran out of space and it was time to rent a small warehouse, I just did it. And then, when we had to add another truck, I just did that. And buy equipment. And put more guys on the payroll. And rent another, bigger warehouse and office space. Then buy more trucks. And then, take on new accounts we didn't have enough men for. And then, buy an office building. And then, buy a bigger house for our growing family. And then, pay guys from our credit card because our clients were behind on paying us. And then, add more employees, and more equipment, and throw employee parties. I just did it. I didn't read a book or consult a consultant. I was a man without a rearview mirror. *God was in control, not me.*

I didn't even know how much money we had, how much we were spending, nor how many employees were on payroll. In 2 Samuel 24, God got mad at King David for counting his men when they weren't his to count. I thought, *Well, my employees aren't mine, so I don't really need to know.* I have no idea if I applied that Bible passage correctly or incorrectly, but that is exactly the point. Whether I got it right, or I blew it completely, it didn't matter. If I was walking in Christ, God promised He would take care of it. The way I saw it, He wasn't there for when you did stuff well. He was there for when you failed, as long as you did it unto Him. After that, it was all in His court. Truthfully, I don't really know if I was acting faithfully, or foolishly. I'm not even sure where one ends and the other begins.

> Working with me was truly like holding onto an unbroken horse.

All I know is this. God had it and still has it. Period.

And while I carried on the way I did, it is not lost on me that I had the perfect accomplice in my wife. Karen was reared in a very conservative home, the daughter of depression-era kids, and raised in the ultra-conservative Quaker church. I had every reason to believe that she would not have the tolerance for my run and gun behavior. Working with me was truly like holding onto an unbroken horse. But, while I was out on the road putting our teams up in hotels and feeding them, charging equipment and materials and adding accounts at a blinding speed, Karen was at home doing the books, taking calls, caring for the kids, making meals, driving to schools and practices, signing loan papers, and sometimes, driving to our clients' offices to pick up checks so we'd have enough to pay our guys—who I promised would get checks every week. When I asked her to meet our payroll by putting the whole thing on our credit card, she just did it. When I asked her to go into debt to cover a commitment I had made to help fund a ministry at church, she did that too. It got inside of her just like it did with me. The idea of growing a business and then giving away so much of the profit just to see God bless us with even more growth got to be thrilling—a bona fide adrenaline rush.

Once, when I asked her why she went along with my crazy ideas, her answer was reminiscent of the kinds of things she said early on in our relationship when I fell in love with her. "I was taught to follow my husband's leadership as an act of obedience to God," she said. "I felt God had given you a vision for

MBW and my responsibility was to support you in every way."

Truthfully, Karen's willingness to hold onto my leash while I dragged her around is a miracle and testimony to her faith. She bought into our Lord's promise to set us free to risk it all—because *having* it all was never the goal. I fully believe that if everything we worked for went away and we suddenly found ourselves living in a little one-bedroom apartment in a bad part of town, she would be content. I know I would be. I think we'd both look at each other and say, *Thank you, Lord. It was a great ride.*

FOR REFLECTION

Faith in Christ is a license to risk. This can be a difficult path, and even more so if your spouse does not support it. Are you and your spouse in sync on some of the big questions with respect to your business, such as, whose business it *really is?* Or, whose money it *really is?*

I've seen many people struggle and fail in business because they aren't getting support from their spouse. How do you think you and your spouse can come into alignment with the direction God might be leading your business? By Bible study? Prayer? A commitment to submitting all things to Him? All of the above?

Could it be that your next most urgent business decision may have to do with your marriage? What would that look like? What steps could be taken?

9

The Banquet

I WAS STILL ASLEEP THE MORNING that my eyes suddenly flipped open as if *being awake* wasn't what it was that drew my eyelids apart, but the sudden remembrance of what I had done the night before. I had asked Jesus—God Almighty—to come into my heart and save me from the pain and hopelessness of my life. And He did.

So, I blinked in the early sunlight of my room and felt the physical movement of my eyes moving back and forth. It was real. It wasn't a dream. I was saved.

And, *I felt so grateful.*

"Thank you, God," I said. "Thank you, thank you." I got up and looked in the mirror, smiled and shook my head. "Thank you," I said again. I got dressed and walked outside to start my day, and would you know it, the day looked to be so full of promise, even under the marine layer that grays the Southern California days each June. And I said it again.

It seemed that it was all I could say.

> I was different now that I had a Savior. I was grateful.

It was then, in the middle of that morning, that I noticed something about me that I hadn't before. Yes, I was different now that I had a Savior, but it was something more. I *was grateful*. In all my life, I don't know that I had ever had a real moment of feeling gratitude. It was as if this feeling was somehow a new expression, or a brand new language that I was suddenly fluent in. And, it felt oddly good.

Thank you, Lord.

I tried to think back to a time when I felt thankful about anything that had happened to me. I know there were good things that occurred, such as winning at sports, receiving a gift, or a nice word, or whatever. But now that I felt genuinely grateful, it didn't seem remotely familiar. Could I have really gone through the first eighteen years of my life and never felt gratitude?

I had always worn my meager life like a lead coat. I hated my small house, my small street, and my neighborhood filled with small-minded people. I hated that my dad left me, and the only, constant voice in my ear was that of my mother who never had a moment for me, or the inclination to try to make friends with me. *She was just Mom. Period. Deal with it. Don't like what she has to say? Tough.*

I hated that I had to work and get myself by when some of my friends were getting cars as they turned 16. When I got a paycheck from the chicken place or the surplus store or wherever, I wasn't grateful for it. The way I saw it, I was doing them a favor. Besides, the checks were barely big enough to do anything with. What was there to be grateful for? *I worked my tail off for this?*

But, when you live a life like mine, and then Jesus comes in to make all things new, all one can do is whisper, exclaim, or scream, *Thank you, thank you, thank you!* To me, being saved meant *I was really being saved*, like a hand pulling me off a cliff. I was saved from being mad forever, from being alone, high, directionless and lost in the aching emptiness of another, then another, conquest.

And now that I was safe in the embrace of Christ, everything was different. But it was just getting started.

As I mentioned before, one of the unique aspects of the beginning of my walk with Jesus was that so much of the initial delving into the Bible was done as a group. Together, with all my new brothers in Christ, we read and spurred each other on, and the more amazing things we discovered, the more we wanted to share, and the more we shared, the more excited we became, and the more excited we became, the more we fell in love with Jesus. It was truly a transformative period in my life. During that time, we happened upon a story in the Gospel of Luke, and it made my heart swell.

There, in chapter seventeen, ten lepers saw Jesus and, staying at a safe distance, called out to Him to have pity on them. Jesus told them to show themselves to the priest, and as they did, He healed them all.

Later on, one of the cleansed men, a Samaritan, came back to find Jesus. When he did, he threw himself at the feet of Jesus and gave praise. Later in the story, Jesus remarked on the fact that although ten lepers were healed, only one came back to praise the Healer.

That was me. I was the grateful leper, elated to be clean and saved, holding onto one of my Lord's ankles.

I walked through the day with so much joy knowing that all my sins, my past, my baggage, every shameful act—no longer applied to me. I felt like I was on the moon, barely held down by gravity. And when I ran into people I knew, they saw a different person. I was just like my brother Paul when he arrived home from camp, a new and different kid—all joyous and smiley. I couldn't hold it back either. Gratitude was coming out of my pores.

I guess I really, really didn't like my life.

The gratitude never seemed to go away. I had new friends, a new love of my life—Karen, new rock and roll bands to become a fan of, new experiences, and new issues that occupied my mind. The best part was every time I turned around, there was another reason from right there in the Bible to fall in love with God *all over again*.

Thank you, Lord.

In fact, years later, when Sam tried to stick me with nothing as we went our separate ways, even then gratitude was never far from me. I remember the odd feeling of not being vengeful for his spiteful ways, but rather grateful that I had so much time with him—he taught me everything about the business I was about to embark on.

And, when I did start MBW, the majority of the guys I hired were living below the poverty level—immigrants and guys out of the barrios. All those hard working faces reminded me of the story in Luke chapter fourteen where a man prepared a huge banquet. He ordered his servant to go out and tell his invited guests to come because the banquet was ready. But each of them had something else that required their attention at that moment and they could not make it to the party. So, the man filled the tables with the poor, crippled, blind and lame and enjoyed their company instead.

I was grateful to work with guys that were lowly in the eyes of society. And, from the gratitude that was spilling over the banks of my heart, I gave each of them a large helping. In fact, I told them relentlessly how much I appreciated their being at my job sites, or should I say, my banquet. And that is when something unexpected happened. They started to thank me in reply—sometimes with words, sometimes with something even better: Nearly every one of my guys worked tirelessly, even when I had the crazy notion that we were going to build an empire by out-working and out-servicing all my competition. They could have dropped me to go work for a boss who was much more sane and only wanted them from 7am-3pm instead of the 12-hour days I required. But, they didn't. I paid them above average and I treated them above average, and their own gratitude showed in their joy on the job. Only happy employees would run for me when they could walk for someone else. In fact, many of the guys who started with me all the way back in 1981 are on the payroll even today.

Even my clients knew how grateful I was—because I told them all the time. These guys stuck their necks out for me whenever they gave me a job and I never forgot that. I can't say I remember them telling me in so many words that they felt the same way too, but they didn't have to. Each time they gave me an after-hours or weekend job—and supplied me the combination to the fence locks so I could waltz right in with my guys, and then immediately paid me from the tailgate of their truck instead of 30-60 days later—that was my thanks. I believe that trust is gratitude.

> Today, I am convinced that gratitude creates its own synergy.

Today, I am convinced that gratitude creates its own synergy. The more you thank someone, the more they feel valued—and personal value is many times greater than the value of a paycheck. Once a person feels like they are getting that need met, they will do anything to please you. I get the sense that CEOs who spend a lot of money on workplace perks could save a lot by just employing this simple concept: Look them in the eye and say I appreciate your hard work. You are an asset. *We're a better place with you here.*

And see if it isn't true: Success follows gratitude.

But of course, you'd have to feel it to say it. And I certainly did and do. No manipulation of feelings, here. I meant every word of it. I felt every word of it. I was every word of it.

Thank you, Lord.

I think that's what opened my eyes so abruptly that first morning. Beneath it all, it was gratitude surging through my veins.

FOR REFLECTION

If you are not someone who is consistently full of thankfulness for your new life in Christ, ask yourself, why? What are some steps you can take to bring about gratitude more consistently?

Do you think your circumstances should play a role in your level of gratitude? See, James 1:2-4 (NASB): "Consider it all joy, my brethren, when you encounter various trials, knowing that the testing of your faith produces endurance. And let endurance have its perfect result, so that you may be perfect and complete, lacking in nothing."

In an honest assessment of your life, of all the things you are most grateful for, where does the Cross of Christ rank?

10

Visitor to the Palace

I LOOKED AT IT AS IT PASSED IN FRONT OF ME. The crumpled bill my dad dropped in the offering plate sat creased and looked a bit sad.

As a little kid in Catholic mass alongside my parents, I was always one to notice the journey that the bill had taken. I watched as it traveled from the inside of my dad's sat-upon wallet as he freed it from the left suit pant pocket, to his lap as he leafed through the bills to find the right one, to between his two fingers as he breathed deeply and then gave it a quick, short ride…with a flick…into the plate. And there it was.

Offering.

I wasn't really clear on the whole offering thing: why we did it and where it was going. The funny thing was, I never heard the priest talk about it. I was on the lookout for it, too, trying to hear a little something about why, each Sunday, the plate snaked its way through the church and filled up with all those bills. All I knew was that as Catholics, it was as much a part of our Sunday service as Mary, the mother of Christ, and the crucifixion.

> I was trying to hear a little something about why, each Sunday, the plate snaked through the church and filled up with all those bills.

So much of my Catholic upbringing led me to a place of wondering *what was the point*. Even in Catholic school, where the mythical stories were geared toward our young minds, they all seemed so, sorry to say, ridiculous. I didn't buy any of it. I remember one, in particular, where a man carried a baby covered in cloths across a great river. When he got to other side, he removed the cloths to find that it was the baby Jesus.

I was completely lost. What was I supposed to get out of that?

Yet, years later, just after giving my life to Christ, when my new friends and I started staying up late into the night reading the Bible, everything on those pages, from the talking donkey, to an adrift animal-filled arc, to the great fish that swallowed a wayward messenger, felt like truth; like, *the sky-is-blue truth*. It just was. But why? They were still mythical, and by the world's standards, crazy-talk stories. What had changed?

Everything.

I hadn't merely come to a change in perspective. My heart had been transformed, and, according to 1 Corinthians 2:16, I had been given the "mind of Christ," which is to say, the ability to understand the Word of God by the power of the Holy Spirit. Suddenly, everything God said through His Word not only felt true, the joy in my heart confirmed it.

So, when God said in the Scriptures, *Trust Me with your life*, I couldn't wait to do it. I wanted to trust Him with everything. Trusting in myself had proven to be a dead end.

It was at this time that Walt Hoffman's influence jumped to a new level. He was asked to take the leadership role at Monday Night Bible Study and so, each Monday night, he taught from the front of the social hall at Alamitos Friends Church. There he was, a straight-laced electrical engineer, black-rimmed glasses and all, standing in front of 300 long-haired teenagers, giving the basics of the Bible and having most of it enthusiastically received—a miracle in and of itself. That's when something rather thunderous happened to me. Walt talked about trusting God in a way that I didn't expect—it had to do with my money. "When you tithe, you're offering God 10% of the first fruits of your labor. What you're saying is, *I trust You with my life, my finances, and my future. Now, how the world sees security no longer applies.*" My eyes and heart lit up—I enjoyed a good, risky adventure now and then. But here's the best part: tithing was not a component of faith, but central as if inextricably tied. According to Walt, to trust God with your heart and life, and not trust Him with your money, made no sense whatsoever. If you did one without the other, it was time for some serious self-reflection.

NOT MY BUSINESS

I love how all-or-nothing our faith is.

I was like, *Great, let's do it*, as if it was something to learn once and then go execute. But, the language of trust and forsaking earthly security is laced throughout Scripture. Therefore, it is something to learn about, ponder, exercise daily, and enjoy for a lifetime. For our own freedom, God directs us to grow in trust each day, and He gives us the tools to do it. As we walk with Him daily, we gain the perspective that all our money is His, and to tithe the *first tenth* of our earnings shows that we trust Him with *everything*. This makes God's heart swell because He intends to bless us beyond our wildest dreams. "Honour the LORD with thy substance, and with the firstfruits of all thine increase: So shall thy barns be filled with plenty, and thy presses shall burst out with new wine." Proverbs 3:9-10 (KJV).

I recognize that many—maybe most—Christians regard tithing as a mere part of their faith—just one more thing to keep in mind, like going to church and refraining from cursing. So, it really takes my breath away to think that I was one of the blessed few who, at the very beginning of my faith when I was so in love with Him, didn't even have the lens to question it. I got to hear about God's gift of freedom in the form of tithing—at its core level, the "this-is-what-it's-all-about" stuff. Tithing and trust go hand-in-hand with salvation.

And so, with Karen being my perfect partner, and already a tither, we earned and gave, then earned and gave some more, and then, wouldn't you know it, He seemed to give us more earnings, so we gave it back, and suddenly, it was like playing two-square with God. It was simple and thrilling. And life got fun, maybe even easy.

So many guys I met along the way, real heavy-hitters who made great amounts of money, seemed to worry over every penny. My heart broke for them as money seemed to choke off their joy. All they had to do was believe that none of it was ever theirs. It was all God's, every last red cent. See, Psalm 24:1. So, the pressure they felt, had they chosen a life of disciplined tithing, could have been completely removed. Why do you think Jesus talked so much about money—because He needed it? Or, because He knew it was killing us?

> Financial growth is just one of the blessings I have received. It may be the least of them all.

I believe God is looking for people who want to be a part of His regenerative program—the Trust/Give/Receive His Blessing Program. Will it always come in the form of money? I think you can bet that it will not. While I was given great amounts, if the money was stripped away, all that I would have left would be my lovely wife, my sons, their beautiful families, health, a big Christian extended family, lots of friends, incredible joy, peace, and…

Financial growth is just one of the blessings I have received. It may be the least of them all.

Lastly, Walt, along with his friendship and willingness to share his wisdom, blessed me in one more way. He was, just by watching him, such an example of a transformed heart. When the offering plate came to him, Walt's posture changed. In his own quiet way, he bowed his head, and with two hands just above his lap, held his offering before the Lord and prayed. It was like a visitor to the palace offering a gift at the throne of the King. Walt, a man of great means, was a humble, grateful servant.

It is an indelible image. I so wish my dad could have seen it.

FOR REFLECTION

When Cain and Abel offer sacrifices to God in Genesis 4:3-5, one is rejected and one is accepted. Whose is accepted and why? Does God want a tenth or the first tenth? Is it after taxes or before?

If something happened to the company you worked for and suddenly your paycheck was cut in half, do you believe God would still require you to tithe even if your checks no longer covered your bills? What do you believe God is after, your money or your trust? If God is your Savior, what should your perspective be on what the world says is wise use of your money? Do you have any perspectives on money that might need to be reconsidered? Which ones?

11

Wink and a Nod

"DUDE, I HAVE TO CREW UP FOR A JOB that we need to work this Sunday," I said into the phone to my brother, Willie, who was one of my regular guys, "I need you on a ladder. You in?"

After he said yes, I hung up the phone, and slowly stood and looked around, trying to see if a dark cloud might descend on me. I watched and waited. But there was nothing—and nothing was a miracle. I felt no guilt about what I had just done. In fact, I felt a bit of joy. *Could it really be?*

It had been a long journey to that place of freedom. And it almost never happened.

It started when I was in the first grade, the day of my first confessional. I was inside the confession booth, within the majestic walls of St. Barbara's Church, nervously waiting on the priest to do what I had been told he would. And then suddenly, it happened. He slid the small door open, and I saw his dimly-lit face obscured by the screen that separated us. Then I gulped, made the sign of the cross, and spoke. "Bless me, Father," I said in my quivering six-year-old voice, "for I have sinned."

"Go ahead, my son," the priest said as if he was expecting a long list.

This was the part, I was told, where if I revealed to this man what I had done wrong, that I would be absolved of my sin, the condemnation of God would pass by me, and I could avoid hell. That sounded pretty good to me. So, I laced together a few good ones, including fighting, hitting, talking back and a couple of other sins that I hoped, by offering to the priest, would keep me away from the fiery gates.

He asked me to say a few Hail Mary's and it all seemed to be going pretty well, even ending a little quicker than I thought. I was about to step out of the confession booth when suddenly the priest said the words that echoed in my ears as I walked away. "Now go and sin no more."

It was as if I got clean and dirty in the same moment. I was cleansed of my sins through confession, but in a single breath I was condemned to go and live a life that didn't sound possible, probable, or frankly, real. I was a six-year-old boy with brothers to fight, a fiery mom to keep off my back, and best friends who, along with me, liked to get into a lot of trouble every time we had the chance. And, the priest wanted me to go and do what?

In the years ahead, my Catholic teachers beat the drum relentlessly about our susceptibility to sin, both mortal and venial, which caused me to vigilantly consider where my sins fell and whether I deserved purgatory or worse. I desperately wanted to be a good boy, and yet *good* seemed to be at the surface of an ocean that I was anchored firmly beneath.

> My mind would conjure violent acts of vengeance when a nun would smack me around.

And yet, try as I did to follow the faith in the years to come, confession after confession the priest would torpedo me with those same six words, "Now go and sin no more." They would make me stiffen. *It seemed impossible.* Regularly, my mind would conjure violent acts of vengeance when a nun would smack me around, and I had buddies who wanted to talk about everything that would make a priest blush. There were also lots of girls in plaid skirts who wanted to get my attention. That was the worst of all. They would walk up, brush against me and suddenly that feeling firing through my body was another sin? Are you kidding me?

I was sunk. There was no winning for me. I was standing in line headed for purgatory. Confession had become a brittle, awful, confusing ritual that left me feeling like nothing more than a minute-by-minute failure.

Now go and sin no more.

Sunday mass was also an awful heel on the back of my neck. With "Keeping the Sabbath Day Holy" an actual Commandment, the nuns made it very clear that to miss mass was to commit a mortal sin—deserving of hell.

"Always attend mass," Sister Dombrowski said with a finger wag. "If you don't, Father McConahey will know."

It was all too much. Not only did I have to deal with the feeling of *not* wanting to go to mass, I really just wanted to run as far away as possible. And so, I did.

Over time, I became a solace junkie—I just needed something to take away the dull ache of constant guilt—and I found it in boards, babes, and bags of pot. I wasn't strong enough to be a Catholic, and I burned my bridge to God every day, hoping someone or something would come along—like the discovery of an ancient tablet—and finally inform the world that whoops, all this mortal sin stuff was just a terrible mistake, and everything would be OK. In the meantime, I was screwed.

That is why when Walt Hoffman presented me with the *forgiveness* of Christ, it was so mind-bending and so attractive—because it seemed so unconditional. *That can't be right, can it?* I didn't know it but God was presenting Himself to me in a one-two punch, and two was about to happen.

It occurred when Walt took a bunch of us guys to a Billy Graham Crusade in Anaheim. That is where it seemed the Cross of Christ stretched into the night sky and loomed large over me like it was asking, even daring me to latch on; to trust. "Because of the Cross, you are forgiven," Billy said. "Think your sins are too much, too bad, too many to be forgiven? You're wrong. The Cross says *not so*. The blood of Jesus reaches you, even you, right where you are. Romans 8 says, 'there is now no condemnation for those who are in Christ Jesus,' and that, nothing can 'separate us from the love of God.' Did you hear that, friends? Nothing."

Nothing? Not my past, my present, and not my future? Not my venial or mortal sins and not even my fading interest in pleasing my priest, or my inconsistent attendance at confession or mass, or my incredibly consistent attendance at all the things I should have never been doing? *Nothing?*

I remember the feeling like it was yesterday. It was as if I had finally breached the ocean's surface after a lifetime of being pushed to the bottom, and now, in the beautiful, sweet oxygen of forgiveness, I gasped my way back to life. I was free. I walked away, lighter than air with this one solitary thought: I couldn't heap on the guilt if I wanted to. Praise God. Let the tears roll.

Some years later, when I tried to bring my company under Sam and he accused me of trying to steal his customers, our split left me with nothing; no money, none of the business I had built up; he even took my truck. When word got out that I was on my own, suddenly, old and new customers began to call, and I began to get jobs. Some of them were on the weekends—including Sundays. And, wouldn't you know it, the old reflexes were there, little moments of doubt, wondering if I was doing the right thing by accepting work on a Sunday and not going to church.

But, this made me recall the time in Matthew 12 where Christ's disciples plucked the grain from the field as they walked through, and ate it. The Pharisees, knowing that it all was occurring on a Sabbath day, saw a breach of the Commandment—and threw a flag. *Aha! No working on the Sabbath! You, Jesus, couldn't possibly be who you say you are if your disciples act like that! What do you have to say for yourself?*

The first thing that Jesus did was to site their hero, King David, and remind them of the time that he broke the rules by allowing his men to eat the consecrated bread in the House of God.

Oh.

Jesus' goal in the rest of Matthew 12 was to say, *You've taken all of God's love, and you made rules out of it— rules to pin people down, rules to use as leverage, rules to secure your own power. I never wanted your rules. The Sabbath was for you. I just wanted a relationship.*

> I whole-heartedly believe in keeping the Sabbath.

I whole-heartedly believe in keeping the Sabbath. I believe that in the Sabbath, God is giving us a bit of Himself, His righteous character for our good. That is why I initially felt a little awkward about working on a Sunday. But, when I thought about what God gave David to do, such as defend Israel, I simply can't believe that if his army was attacked on the Sabbath, he laid down his sword.

I believe he fought.

In the same way, I really felt that God was giving me my life's work when all those calls started to come. The work wasn't coming on the weekdays but on the weekends. I could have said no, but suddenly the dull thud of a rule clanked against my soul. It just didn't feel right to say no. *To say no felt like I didn't know my God at all.*

> Best of all, I didn't, not for one second, feel condemnation from God. I felt free.

And the strangest thing happened after I began to take the Sunday jobs. No one, not my Monday Night Bible Study friends, or Walt, or the pastor of our church, or Karen or her parents or anyone associated with my new life in Christ raised so much as an eyebrow. No one called, warned, and no fingers were wagged. Best of all, I didn't, not for one second, feel condemnation from God. I felt free. I felt forgiven. I felt like God gave me a wink and a nod, if you want to know the truth.

I felt so in love with God that I couldn't wait to go back to church. Now, it was a matter of growing the business large enough to make some space for me to do just that. So, we started making new processes and innovations in how we operated, and suddenly, we transitioned into a well-oiled caulking machine the likes of which nobody had seen before. We became legendary all over the West coast. We used to jump out of our trucks like ants with guys climbing up ladders, other guys running material back and forth in a sprint, and other guys filling guns. Our crews were bouncing off the walls, going up and down and around the corners until all that was seen of us was a cloud of dust. The whole building was done in a blur.

Next!

And of course, when MBW got on its feet, I went back to church and lavished in a God who could love me enough to forgive me now, always, no matter what. Try as I might to take back the guilt, the matter was over.

Many years later, I threw a big party and included all the guys who worked alongside me in those early years to grow MBW into one of the largest caulking and waterproofing companies in the West. In the invitation, I quoted 2 Samuel 23 where David honors the mighty warriors who fought alongside him. In my own way, I wanted to do the same thing—but with a bit of a twist. Known only to me, I was honoring and giving thanks to my God who, by His unspeakable grace, cared nothing about the rule, and only about the relationship.

FOR REFLECTION

Do you think it is common that most of us still cloud the forgiveness we have in Christ with man-made rules? What can we do to truly live free? What rules do you apply to your own faith that just might need reconsideration? When you compare the forgiveness that Christ won for us on the Cross, to sin, which has more power?

Read Matthew 18:21-22.

Is keeping the Sabbath Day merely a good idea, a wise suggestion, or part of God's character and gift to you? See Genesis 2:2. Why did God give us the Sabbath Day to keep holy?

12

Three in the Pocket

1. Treat everyone the same

2. Make your bosses look good to their bosses

3. Show gratitude

IT WAS A PARTICULARLY HOT DAY. I had been out in the sun ever since it popped up over the mountains and started to burn on the desert where we were working. I had polished off my water bottle early, by about 10:30. I was near, let's call it, the, "Smith and Jones Construction" trailer, and ducked inside to get a drink. That's when one of their young, 20-something college grad supervisors saw me, a sweaty laborer, or so he thought, inside *their domain*.

"Nah, you guys don't belong in here," he said. "You get water from the outside." And so, without making a stink about it, I put down the paper cup and made my way out the door. What he didn't know was that I was the owner of MBW, and friends with the owner of his company. Had he known, is there any question that he would have treated me differently?

It was cultural with Smith and Jones. I had seen them in action on many occasions, all their young supervisors just out of business school treating the low-level guys with disdain. They knew the pecking order, and as a matter of business, they believed the riff raff laborers needed to be bullied for the work to get done efficiently. But it didn't stop there. Every interaction between supervisor and worker was out of balance, with the young bucks in ties holding all the power. And so they lauded it over them, and me. It was really bad.

I recalled my early days, after coming to know Christ, when I read Romans 2:11 and was elated to learn that *"God is no respecter of persons."* I was from my community's cheap seats, the bluest of blue-collar neighborhoods. Little ugly houses, tight streets, and kids left alone so moms could go to work. It wasn't the slums, but it was basic poor—a no-frills life—and I felt it.

And just in case there was any confusion about my place in the world, all I had to do was go to surf spots in Huntington or Newport Beach where the homes were huge. The rich and important people treated us hoi polloi like they would a stray dog sniffing at their bushes. So when I found out that God did not see a difference between me and the powerful, that He loved us all equally, it was another reason to give Him my heart and be filled with gratitude. I wasn't happy that those folks were brought down to size. I was just happy that my low standing wasn't a notch against me. God loved me as much as He did any man—and considering His death on the Cross, it was a level of love I'll never fully comprehend.

One of the most compelling stories in the Bible is the woman at the well in John 4. Jesus sits, talks and receives water from a woman who was not just from the wrong side of the tracks, but was from a people the Jews did not associate with. But it was worse than that. This particular woman was an outcast even in her own community. And yet, Jesus offers her Living Water, which is to say, *Himself*. Her lowest-of-the-low social standing mattered not a whit. He loved her.

That's why on the job sites, and everywhere in life, I've always treated people with respect and kindness, whether they were wearing a tie or tar. I made friends with everyone, from the company owners to the general contractors to the sack and patch guys. And I truly believe, in the hierarchy-addled industry of construction, people noticed. As I led by example, I believe it rubbed off on my guys. I began to notice that the sack and patchers, who were mostly made up of the Mexican guys from the barrios, would start to close the distance between them and us. They could see we were a friendly bunch and it must have felt good to be welcomed by guys who normally didn't do that.

In the end, it seemed to ingratiate MBW with a lot of people who were instrumental in offering work at a time when we really needed it. It was the period when I had split from Sam and was in a scramble to get as much work as I could—from anywhere I could find it. About that time, some of the concrete guys who hired caulkers would try to get a better price by hiring some of the sack and patch guys to do the caulking

> Kindness, in itself, is its own reward.

on their jobs. The sack and patchers were the guys who knew me from the other job sites, and had come to like me enough to give me the nickname: *Ojos Azul*. If they found the caulking work to be more difficult than expected, or just not fitting with their timetable, that's when they would call me. The jobs were small, but they were essential to keeping MBW alive. If I hadn't treated these guys with respect and kindness, I don't think the calls would have come.

While it did benefit me to be kind to all people, even those who are not, kindness, in itself, is its own reward. Obedience blesses the Lord, you, and the folks you're kind to. There is no losing with kindness.

IF I WERE TO WRITE DOWN THE JOB DESCRIPTION OF A CAULKER, it would be a rather quick read: *To lay a strip of caulking material between two sections of newly constructed wall at the point where they come together.* Give or take, that's about it.

That's what I did every day and that's what I taught my guys to do. But one day, that job description changed.

It was the day that a supervisor took me out to where I had just finished caulking a wall and asked me to look at it again. "See the way this section protrudes a couple of inches from the other section? You just caulked straight across, leaving this lip of wall—and it doesn't look good. It creates a shadow. Can't you lay your caulking so it goes at an angle and makes the wall look a little more finished?"

Was this guy kidding? These guys do a lousy job of tilting these walls, and he wants me to make it look better? I had every right to say, *Not my job, man.* To beautify his poorly erected walls would mean more time, and time is money. Not to mention it would take more material. I had a business to run at a profit, and a wife and kids to get home to. I wasn't about to take on his problem.

Suddenly, I remembered Colossians 3:23-24: "And whatever you do, do it heartily, as to the Lord and not to men, knowing that from the Lord you will receive the reward of the inheritance; for you serve the Lord Christ." (NKJV).

I looked at the guy standing there chatting away about the need for a more deft hand at caulking and I thought to myself, *Boy, did you just ask the right guy*—because I changed that day. I absolutely was going to help make the building look better because in this job, just like every job I ever had, God was my ultimate boss. I was working for Him. Why would I not heartily give of my time and talent when the One I was trying to please was the Lord Himself?

And so, I began to feather the caulking material to hide all the sharp edges and create a clean look whenever there was the need. And you know what? It began to look rather beautiful—to me! I was eager to do it anytime I could. The pride I took in my work skyrocketed. God was changing everything about me—the way I worked, and even the way I saw my work. *It was thrilling.*

Add to that, my supervisors—the concrete guys who hired me, or the general contractors, had nothing but words of praise for my work. I'm not even sure they knew that I was smoothing out the walls. I didn't feel the need to toot my own horn and bring my above-par work to their attention. They just knew that the facades were looking good. That was enough for me. It feels great to make someone else look good to their bosses or the customers they work for. That is reward enough. And you know what? Going that extra mile did take more time and money, but it brought me so much more work that I came out way ahead.

Every job you have, everywhere you go, there are walls that are out of alignment—so to speak; opportunities to smooth something over, make it look more beautiful or function better than it did a moment ago—not because you'll look good, but because you're helping to make your boss look good. It seems to me to be perfectly in line with what God is asking you to do by working unto Him. If you work as if He is your boss, you heap flowers upon someone else's head. That kind of grace, whether your supervisor deserves it or not, is the kind of thing every workplace could use. And you're going to feel good about it.

My new job description for a caulker: *To lay a strip of caulking material between two sections of newly constructed wall at the point where they come together—whether they actually come together or not.*

I HAVE WORKED FOR SOME OF THE WORST MANAGERS, foremen, supervisors and GCs imaginable. They have no people skills, yet they run teams of people. They believe that to scream and yell, push as hard as possible, and, disregard of a person's humanity for the sake of the job is the way to get stuff done. They degrade, they insult, they are consistently disrespectful to the people they manage. You can't stand to be around them, and you look for just the right time to tell them a piece of your mind—but it rarely comes. I know. I've been there.

You probably expect me to suggest that you hold your tongue when you come across someone like that. But I won't. Holding your tongue doesn't change your heart. It just leaves you silently mad, hurt and dreading the next day's work.

The book of James says to "Consider it all joy… when you encounter various trials." James 1:2-4 (NASB). That is not a snappy, homespun quip for a framed needlepoint. Nor is it a suggestion. James is telling you to make a paradigm shift—for your own good.

Paul said in Philippians, "Do nothing from selfishness or empty conceit, but with humility of mind regard one another as more important than yourselves; do not merely look out for your own personal interests, but also for the interests of others." Philippians 2:3 (NASB).

When you come under the supervision of a tyrant, look out for his interests before yours. Be grateful, and show him gratitude. Watch how it blesses him, and at the same time, neutralizes his affect on you. It lightens your step. You will do better work. It will ingratiate him to you, and you may start to see him change. He may even ask you to do more of his jobs—everyone, even tyrants, want to work with a cheerful guy.

But, gratitude should not be a matter of strategy. Instead, *be grateful* for the work. The job could have gone to someone else, and you could be at home watching TV, waiting by the phone and sweating out next month's bills. But, you're not. You're working, being productive, making money. Be grateful and let it show. It has the potential to change everything: your heart, the supervisor, and your future.

FOR REFLECTION

Proverbs 22:29 says, "See a man who is skilled in his trade, he will stand before kings." This verse motivated me to be the best at what I do, because if I were, there would be reward for me, some way, somehow.

Think of Joseph and his incredible skill for interpreting dreams. He eventually stood before the most powerful man on earth—the king of Egypt. Ultimately, the king put him in charge of his kingdom where Joseph stockpiled grain in preparation for a famine. When the famine came, it made Egypt the richest country on the planet. And perhaps, just behind the king, Joseph was the most powerful man on earth.

Going back to when Joseph was just a boy, he had big dreams, for sure. But even he couldn't have dreamed that God would take him to the stratospheric heights that He did.

Are you being the best that you can be at what you do? Are you prepared to stand before the King? What action steps can you take to be even better than you currently are at what you do?

13

The Close One

GENESIS 22 (NIV)

"Some time later God tested Abraham. He said to him, 'Abraham!'

'Here I am,' he replied.

Then God said, 'Take your son, your only son, whom you love—Isaac—and go to the region of Moriah. Sacrifice him there as a burnt offering on a mountain I will show you.'

Early the next morning Abraham got up and loaded his donkey. He took with him two of his servants and his son Isaac. When he had cut enough wood for the burnt offering, he set out for the place God had told him about. On the third day Abraham looked up and saw the place in the distance. He said to his servants, 'Stay here with the donkey while I and the boy go over there. We will worship and then we will come back to you.'

Abraham took the wood for the burnt offering and placed it on his son Isaac, and he himself carried the fire and the knife. As the two of them went on together, Isaac spoke up and said to his father Abraham, 'Father?'

'Yes, my son?' Abraham replied.

'The fire and wood are here,' Isaac said, 'but where is the lamb for the burnt offering?'

Abraham answered, 'God himself will provide the lamb for the burnt offering, my son.' And the two of them went on together.

When they reached the place God had told him about, Abraham built an altar there and arranged the wood on it. He bound his son Isaac and laid him on the altar, on top of the wood. Then he reached out his hand and took the knife to slay his son. But the angel of the Lord called out to him from heaven, 'Abraham! Abraham!'

'Here I am,' he replied.

'Do not lay a hand on the boy,' he said. 'Do not do anything to him. Now I know that you fear God, be cause you have not withheld from me your son, your only son.'

Abraham looked up and there in a thicket he saw a ram caught by its horns. He went over and took the ram and sacrificed it as a burnt offering instead of his son. So Abraham called that place The Lord Will Provide. And to this day it is said, 'On the mountain of the Lord it will be provided.'

The angel of the Lord called to Abraham from heaven a second time and said, 'I swear by myself, declares the Lord, that because you have done this and have not withheld your son, your only son, I will surely bless you and make your descendants as numerous as the stars in the sky and as the sand on the seashore. Your descendants will take possession of the cities of their enemies, and through your offspring all nations on earth will be blessed, because you have obeyed me.'

Then Abraham returned to his servants, and they set off together for Beersheba. And Abraham stayed in Beersheba.

CONSIDERING THE NUMBER OF CHILDREN who grow up to be adults with serious emotional problems because their dad was not home, not attentive, or died early, but for Jesus calling me to Himself, *it could have happened to me*. I look back and think, *Whew. That was a close one.*

I have talked with others, and it is a very common thing: When one parent dies young, there is something that happens inside the heart and mind of a child that prevents them from being able to project their life in the future. I think it is for the protection of one's own psyche. I'll explain.

I never saw myself growing up past my teen years, getting married, settling down, and I certainly never saw myself having children. It wasn't that I chose not to think about it, it just wasn't there. It was as if my dad's death clipped my ability to think of the future as he fell past and away from my life. They both seemed to die that day.

Years later, when my sons, Adam and Blake were born, an amazing thing happened. It wasn't just a matter of receiving their lives into mine, but in a way, I was receiving a bit of my life back. The love and gratitude I felt created a tectonic shift in my heart.

I often thought about the story in Genesis, when God tells Abraham and Sarah that He would deliver to them a son, even in their very old age, and Sarah simply couldn't believe it. Her story may not have been exactly like mine, but we shared the same conclusion: how could something like that happen to me? And when it did…well, let's just say, I felt her level of elation.

I love my boys beyond what I can express. Their births were life-changing for me on a spiritual level. Not only had I witnessed a miracle with each of their births, but God actually allowed me to participate in the miracles—and it is truly unbelievable. Even so, I had come to feel that God had given me MBW to run and grow. I knew that Karen was an exceptional mom, so I felt good about leaving them with her, freeing me up to spend nearly seven days a week building the business for my

> Help! Help! Somebody, please help my son!

family. The way I saw it, the more guys I could employ, the more insulated I would be if the economy went bad again. So, I worked it hard.

Even so, I was an attentive dad when time allowed. Karen and I took the kids to Hawaii on a couple of occasions and had a blast. There was one problem, however. It seemed like whenever there was a close call with one of the boys, it was when they were alone with me. Both times something horrifying happened, it was to Blake, my youngest son. On one occasion, I took Blake and Adam to Disneyland along with my brother Paul, and his sons. We were eating at the Tomorrowland Restaurant when all of a sudden Blake started gasping for air when a hot dog lodged in his throat. I started patting him on the back and tried to talk him through getting some air, and it just wasn't happening. I started to panic, and then he did, too, and I could see that he was starting to turn blue. I was yelling at him, *Blake, Blake,* when all of a sudden I found myself shrieking, *Help! Help! Somebody, please help my son!* I noticed the employees starting to run around but nobody was approaching. Suddenly, a tourist jumped out of nowhere, grabbed Blake from behind, and in the blink of an eye, got him into position to administer a swift Heimlich maneuver—and out popped the hotdog.

I was a mess. That hotdog turned the happiest place on earth into a nightmare. When I finally gathered myself enough to be able to talk, I turned to thank the guy. He was nowhere to be found.

An angel?

On another occasion, when Karen stayed home for much-needed rest, I took the boys to my mom's house where she was having a get-together for relatives. Adam and Blake were running in and around the house when suddenly, there was a loud crash. I turned to see that Blake had run through the sliding glass door at full speed. His little body was lacerated nearly everywhere. He spent agonizing weeks of recovery lying on the couch at home covered in stitches like randomly laid train track running up and down his body. It was awful.

My poor track record with the boys is what put me on guard on a spring day in 1991. We were in Brian Head, Utah, skiing with the Pughs, our friends from church, and it was the last run of the last day of a weeklong trip. Karen stayed in the lodge that day as she felt a cold coming on and wanted to rest up for the long trip home. The boys, now 8 and 6, skied well all week, and were excited to ski one more time, so that is why I had them on the hill—alone—around 3PM, for our last run before hitting the lodge and getting on the road.

As we stood on the ledge of the run, the boys decided to get a head start down the hill. I stood and adjusted my equipment and watched them snowplow their way down the clearing that had shadows reaching across it. I wanted to take it all in—it had been a great time in such a spectacular setting. That's when I saw Blake do what brothers do. He skied in front of Adam and cut him off just for the fun of it. Adam, without turning or flinching or even putting up a hand to brace himself, skied straight into a tree, face first, and then plopped back onto the snow. It was as if someone had thrown a large, person-sized beanbag against the tree—a dull collision and lifeless collapse. It was surreal. Did I see what I think I just saw?

I skied down to Adam to take a look. For as hard as he hit the tree, he seemed to be okay. I brushed him off and looked at him closely. He was hurt and crying but doing pretty well for someone who had just been blindsided by a tree. I saw no blood, and he didn't appear to have any broken bones. The only injury I could see was nothing more than what appeared to be bark-burn around his brow.

A woman, who happened to be a nurse, had seen the whole thing and came over to lend a hand. She checked Adam out and seemed to concur with me that he appeared to be fine. When the ski patrol arrived, they also agreed. Before leaving, they offered to drive us to the hospital for one last look. It didn't seem necessary; yet, as I thought about it and looked at Adam, his condition didn't seem consistent with what I just saw happen to him. He had to be more hurt than this after hitting a tree that hard. I agreed we should go to the doctor.

At the bottom of the hill, we were loaded into an ambulance. Adam still seemed to be fine, so now it was just a matter of getting a doctor to sign off and relieve me of any undue concern. All of a sudden, Adam began to vomit. I quickly took him in my arms. Confusion blew through me. *What's this about?* I asked myself.

The answer came right away as Adam began to vomit blood. My boy was in trouble.

When we arrived at the hospital, we were seen quickly and

x-rays of his head were taken. The doctor didn't have a lot to offer other than to say that it was bad, and anything that Adam needed couldn't be done at that facility. I pressed him for more. "Skull fracture around his eye socket and his forehead," he said. I felt myself go weak-kneed.

"You've got two options," he offered. "We can Life Flight him to a larger hospital in Las Vegas, or to one in Salt Lake City. Which do you want?" *Life Flight? Did he say, Life Flight?* It was all starting to feel like a very bad dream. Perhaps it was the fact that this was an extraordinary situation that I did what I did next, or maybe it was because God stepped in, but what I said next is about as unlike me as anything I have ever uttered. I tend to make decisions quickly and boldly. Las Vegas was the obvious location for Adam to be flown as it was closest to our home in Orange County. But, I turned to the doctor and asked, "What would you do if it was your kid, Doc?"

What would HE do? I don't really care what other people would do. I'm the kind of guy who lives rather easily with my decisions, good or bad. I don't really seek out advice. I'm just not that careful. But that is what I asked him. And when he gave his answer, I took it as *Gospel*. "Primary Children's Hospital is in Salt Lake City. They have a world-renowned head trauma specialist. Without question, I'd go there if it was my son," he said. It was three hours further away from our house in Anaheim Hills. But, it didn't matter. Salt Lake City was a go. Karen arrived at the hospital in time to accompany Adam and a nurse to a nearby airport where Adam was loaded into the small plane that took them to Primary Children's Hospital.

The three-hour drive from Brian Head to Salt Lake City is long enough to take a man who is trying to stay strong in the face of fear, and turn him into a tragic ball of tears. Emotionally, that is the ledge I teetered on. But, John Pugh knew his role immediately, which was to talk me down the entire way there. He prayed with me and spoke encouraging words as I struggled for sanity. I thought about Abraham receiving a word from God that He had something for him to do: to sacrifice his son. Every aspect of the story fired into my brain as the minutes passed and the miles on our odometer gathered. The gut-wrenching demand of God, the inquisitive and innocent eyes of Isaac as Abraham tells him where they must travel, Abraham's placing the wood upon young Issac's back, Abraham's voice as he tells his servants where he and Isaac will go and what they will do: to climb the mountain, praise God, make a sacrifice to Him, and then, return. Did he know? Or was it just a matter of a dad, like me, hoping that his loving, heavenly Father would save his boy?

I, too, believed in a loving Father. Would he take my boy from me now? Or could I depend on Him to find a way out of this, as Abraham seemed to do? Whatever the case, I found myself saying, "God, just like Isaac, you gave Adam to me when I never expected it. If you want him back, I'm just going to trust that you know what you're doing." Tears streamed down my face and my hands grew tired from wringing them together. John drove on and prayed on, using every bit of his energy to call the comforting touch of the Holy Spirit into the car. *I will never be able to thank him enough.*

When I arrived at the hospital, I hustled inside and made it known to the first person I saw who I was and who I needed to see. When I got to Adam's floor, Karen was just walking out of the room and in her swollen eyes was a look that I had never seen before—tired desperation. She hugged me not saying a word. I don't think she could. She walked past me and sat down with her head in her hands. I gulped. Suddenly, without anticipating it, I was walking in that room alone and I knew I wasn't going to like it.

As I opened the door, there was a split second where I thought that I was in the wrong room. I didn't recognize the boy in the bed. Adam's head and face had swelled to three times their size. His lips and nose were disfigured. His right eye was black and his left one was on its way. I held on to the bed rail to keep my knees from giving out.

"Adam," I whispered with tears already streaming down my face. All at once I felt the dam begin to crack. I was about to lose it in front of my boy, who, even with his eyes closed, could have been awake enough to hear his dad come undone at the sight of him. I just couldn't risk it. I waited for a moment, steadied myself as best I could, kissed his forehead and touched his hand—but could not speak. Finally, a frail, *I love you*, made it past my lips. Then I went outside and broke in two like a ship blowing apart.

When the doctor we had gone to that hospital for came out and told us his plan of attack, each word was like an affront, like something ripping away at everything we felt we knew about this life. He would have to cut Adam's skin over the top of his head from ear to ear and pull his scalp down to be able to access and repair the skull fracture around the orbital bone of his right eye. His skull would be held together with screws and plates. Once everything was repaired, the large incision over the top of his head would be stapled closed and hopefully, the healing could begin.

The thought of our beautiful boy's handsome face having to be pulled from his skull like wallpaper from a wall was too much to bear. It reduced him to skin and cartilage and bones—pieces of a body, the loveless mere parts of a human instead of the funny, smart, strong-willed soul we knew as our Adam. *How could this be? He was just a little boy on a beginner's slope.*

Almost as agonizing, was that the surgery could not be done until the swelling in his brain went down. So, Adam would have to lie there in that state for days until his body reversed course. I wasn't sure I would make it the next hour let alone the three days the doctor predicted. It would be the longest three days of our lives.

Finally, Adam's swelling receded and they prepped him for surgery, shaving off his beautiful curls and making him look just awful. My son, frail, scared, disfigured and pathetic, lay on his bed holding my hand as we began our journey down the hall toward the O.R. "You're going to be OK, Adam," I told him, not sure of anything I was saying. His little grip was tight around my thumb. I tried give him a reassuring smile all the while hoping that somehow, something might come and make this all go away, perhaps someone to nudge me awake, or maybe even a ram stepping into the hallway.

Finally, the doors opened and Adam was gone. I crumbled in a ball of tears. I forced my inner voice to speak: *If You have to take him, I'll understand. He was Your boy, to begin with.* Then I thought about Abraham. *How in the world did you trust God that much?*

Karen and I waited together, but also isolated in our own way.

The fear turns you inward, to some degree, as you create a bit of a shell for self-preservation, and push away anything like vulnerability. We both spent time in the chapel, on our knees before God. I thought about what was going on at home, with our church body mobilizing to pray and beg God's healing hand. They are such good people. I don't know what I would have done without knowing they were there.

The doctor would appear every couple of hours to give us updates. I can't really explain what it is like to stand before someone who has your son's life in his hands. He was an extraordinarily heroic figure to me. When he told us he was happy with the progress and Adam was doing well, *thank you* seemed so woefully inadequate, like words without meaning.

While we were happy to hear the good news, we were told that if Adam made it through the recovery and we got him back, he could be a different Adam than we knew and loved. Because the orbital bones fractured inward and punctured his brain, there was a chance that his personality could be altered. His eyesight might also be impaired. His eye might droop. Walking could be an issue if his brain function was compromised. We were certainly not out of the woods by any means.

Eight long hours later, the surgery was over and it was successful. Karen and I were overjoyed, although we knew what lay ahead—a long, painful recovery. Would he be different? Would we be different? In the days and weeks that followed, we stayed at the Ronald McDonald House near Primary Children's Hospital, provided for the parents of sick children. It is tragic to see so many people in the throes of battling for their children's lives. Like us, they were going in and out, back and forth to the hospital and the bedside of their child. How sobering it was to know that many of them would never bring their child out of the hospital again. All that pain is just too much to wrap your head around. In the meantime, we received loving calls and cards from our family and friends back home. Pastor Werhas got Dodger legend, Tommy Lasorda, to send Adam a signed baseball, and Angels catcher, Lance Parish, sent a bat—priceless expressions of love and support.

Finally, it was time to let us take Adam home. We were so excited. He still had quite a way to go with his physical recovery, but as far as his personality or mental state, we never saw any of the things we had been told were a possibility. Our Adam was back, same as before. Karen and I even privately joked that perhaps we might get him back just a little bit less stubborn. But no, he was just as stubborn and set in his ways as he always was. Of course, *we were elated*.

We were also grateful for the treatment we had received by everyone at the hospital in Salt Lake City who, top to bottom, had been on their game, efficient, brilliant and deeply caring. It could not have been a better experience, all things considered. We were so grateful that God had led me to ask that question of the doctor. That could only have been from Him.

Ten days after the surgery, Karen's sister, Laura, flew to Salt Lake City to help bring Adam home on a commercial flight while I would drive our minivan all the way back to Anaheim Hills. By this time, Adam was painfully skinny and frail. With his hair shaved, the scar on top of his head was visible and brutal to look at. His eyes were sad and confused as his body and mind were under the power of the anti-seizure medications.

I knew that anything could happen to him and that the plane ride home could be hard on him. So, as they took off, I jumped in our minivan and got on the freeway. By all estimates, it should have taken me 12 hours to drive home and see him. But, there was no way I could wait that long. While Adam, Karen, and Laura were flying, I was too, averaging about 115 miles per hour all the way from Salt Lake City, Utah to Anaheim Hills, California. If anything was going to go wrong with Adam, I was going to be there.

> Adam would have to go through painful tests to eliminate that diagnosis.

We all arrived safely (and without speeding tickets) to a welcome-home party given by family and friends. We were so relieved and ready to put this terrible accident behind us. But days later, Adam suddenly seemed to be feeling worse. He got a raging fever accompanied by a terrible headache, and we, of course, began to freak out. We immediately took him to CHOC, the local children's hospital. The doctors there thought it might be spinal meningitis, a condition from which there may be no coming back. *Lord, please, no.* Adam would have to go through painful tests to eliminate that diagnosis. *How much pain does our precious boy have to endure?*

Right away, we noticed a difference in the care between the two hospitals. Adam wasn't treated like a little celebrity as he was at the hospital in Salt Lake City, but rather, just a problem to be solved and sent home. Even the different shifts of doctors and nurses seemed to bring about competing theories and suggestions for Adam's treatments. When his fever broke, and the spinal tap came back clear, the diagnosis of spinal meningitis was eliminated. Although he was released to go home, we put Adam in the car and drove straight to the airport. We took him back to Primary Children's Hospital in SLC. We stayed there for another week just to make sure he was out of the woods, and under the care of the top-notch doctors and nurses we trusted.

This time, when we returned home, his recovery went without a hitch except for the long stretch of time it took for him to gain weight, grow hair and look and feel like himself again. When he wanted to play little league baseball, we let him. It was such a sight to see him out in right field, skinny like a twig, almost completely lost in his uniform, and a cap so oversized that it hung down too far to see his eyes. But our beautiful Adam was in there, somewhere, his heart beating the rhythm of the Lord's blessing to us. Our boy was back.

Whew. That was a close one.

POSTSCRIPT

Years later, with Adam fully recovered and doing great, Karen and I took him aside and called attention to his rather wide scar that was easily viewable just above his ears and then disappeared into his thick, curly, black hair. "We are perfectly willing to get that taken care of, Adam," we said. "With plastic surgery, we can have that scar reduced to almost nothing so that it is basically never seen unless someone knows to look for it. So would you like to do that?"

He thought about it for a moment. "No," he said. "I like it because it's a good reminder of what God has done for me. He saved my life."

It is impossible not to be moved by that. After all the pain and fear that Adam experienced, his scar is a monument to God's blessing that he wants to carry with him every day for the rest of his life—his Ebenezer.

1 Samuel 7:12 (NKJV) "Then Samuel took a stone and set it up between Mizpah and Shen, and called its name Ebenezer, saying, 'Thus far the Lord has helped us.'"

POSTSCRIPT 2

If one were to look at the timeline of when MBW really exploded, it happened right about the time of Adam's accident. Here's why. I was with Adam during his accident, surgery, and through his most critical times, which turned out to last a couple of months. This meant I had to delegate all my responsibilities to my guys—the office and field workers. Up to that point, I was in control of everything, and all of a sudden, I had to trust them with everything. The result was immediate, obvious, and life changing. It was a heck of a way to learn a lesson, but one that really needed to be learned. You can't do it all. And until you realize that, you'll never be all you can be.

FOR REFLECTION

An Ebenezer is a commemoration of divine assistance. Do you have anything in your life that acts as a reminder or God's faithfulness? See, Joshua 4:19-24: "On the tenth day of the first month the people went up from the Jordan and camped at Gilgal on the eastern border of Jericho. And Joshua set up at Gilgal the twelve stones they had taken out of the Jordan. He said to the people of Israel, "In the future when your descendants ask their fathers, 'What do these stones mean?' then you shall let your descendants know, 'Israel crossed this Jordan on dry ground.' For the LORD your God dried up the waters of the Jordan before you until you had crossed over. The LORD your God did to the Jordan just what he had done to the Red Sea when he dried it up before us until we had crossed over. He did this so that all the peoples of the earth might know that the hand of the LORD is powerful and so that you might always reverence the LORD your God."

Share with someone examples of God's faithfulness today. What has God done in your life? What has He saved you from? What has He given you that you did not deserve? How would your life be different were it not for Him?

14

Footsteps

TODAY, MARK BEAMISH WATERPROOFING is under new leadership. I retired in 2014 and turned the company, a multi-million dollar concern, over to Adam. At the time of taking the helm, Adam was just 32 years old and hadn't ever run a vacuum cleaner, let alone a company. But, it's just one of those things that I do. I just jump in. Hey, it's gotten me this far.

But, I like where MBW is today. Sure, I might do things differently here and there, but Adam is the right one to lead it, not me. It's a different era, one he's more suited for than me. And when I sit and think about where MBW is now, I can look back and see the faint image of God's footprints leading away and back in time—all the way to the floor of Ranger Boats in Anaheim in 1976, the day my right wrist started to hurt.

At age 22, I had a menial job working for Ranger, a company that made fiberglass fishing and ski boats. As a part of the installation team, I installed the vinyl seats, side rails, engine covers and more. The job required a lot of holding, twisting and turning things with my hands and, as is the case with many injuries, the pain started small. After a while, it was so bad on the inside of my right hand and wrist, I could barely do my job. I was almost useless to the company.

When I went to the doctor, tests showed carpal tunnel syndrome, and I would need an operation. I wasn't expecting that. "So, I'll be as good as new once the operation is over, doc?" I asked him.

He smiled. "As long as you're not doing what you're doing now. I'd find a different line of work if I were you. One where you use your head and not your hands."

Hmm. For a guy with little education, how was that going to happen?

At that time, a friend of mine who I surfed with a lot was getting married to one of the Monday Night Bible Study girls. I was still recovering from my carpel tunnel surgery, so I showed up to the wedding with a huge cast on my wrist. I ended up sitting next to a guy named Art, and as he and I were talking he noticed my cast and asked me about it. As I told him about my recent surgery, I also mentioned my doctor's recommendation to find a job where I use my head and not my hands. Art got a look in his eyes as if a light went on…"*I think I may have something for you.*" Art sold Life Insurance for a company called Equitable of Iowa, and offered to introduce me around his company so I could consider a future as a salesman. I was like, "Sure!"

A few months later, I was an employee of Equitable of Iowa, selling life insurance to every friend I could think of just to avoid making cold calls to strangers. It was at that time that I noticed that John Werhas was invited to lead Bible studies at the company for all interested employees, many of whom were former athletes. He started coming and leading regularly, and that's when I met him. He was a nice, charming guy, and his former Dodger status made me look up to him immediately. He was also a terrific speaker.

Soon after, I quit my job because I was horrible at it, and miserable. How I thought I could make a killing selling insurance with my rather introverted personality is beyond me. So, I left, and in total disregard of my doctor's orders, I took up a career in caulking—a job that requires the use of hands and wrists like no other. But, oh well.

By 1988, Karen and I moved our family to a new house in Anaheim Hills. That's when I heard that John Werhas was the new pastor of Yorba Linda Friends Church, which was near our house. I liked John, and I also felt familiar with the Friends Church having worshiped at Alamitos Friends in Garden Grove during the MNBS days. What's more, Karen and I were still searching for a place to call our church home. So we went to Yorba Linda Friends the very next Sunday and just like that, we felt we had arrived. We were finally home. Little did we know that a golden era was about to begin at the church and in our family.

The years that followed were joyous and exciting. The church was at the beginning stages of incredible growth and effectiveness, and the feeling of being part of something extraordinary was in the air. People were getting saved, lives were being changed, and the church was a place of hope and endless possibility. Programs were springing up, people were free to be creative, ministries were launched and the youth programs were teeming with eager kids because of the fantastic leadership of the children's ministry. We could not have felt happier or more blessed.

> People were getting saved and lives were being changed.

Adding to our delight was the kind of people the church attracted. Many were people of great means and generosity, which enabled the church to dream big in following God's call. And because of John's Dodger past, many pro athletes were members of the church, which added an even greater dimension to the excitement.

Now, before you think I was star struck given my reference to the money and celebrity status at church, let me assure you that wasn't the case. You'll see.

About this time, I was introduced to a guy named Bob Noonan, who had a radio program on a Christian station, and we ended up going to different sporting events together, talking about sports and teams the whole time. Bob took me aside one day. "Hey Mark," he said, "I need a sports guy on my show—you know, an analyst of sorts to give a report and engage in some banter. How would you like to be him?"

I quickly thought that with all the conversations that we had about sports, I must have really impressed him. It was either that or I was the only guy who said yes to his offer. But no matter, I was about to do something that had been on my mind since I was a kid listening to Vin Scully on the radio. I was about to be in *sports*.

The gig plunged me even further into the world of high-powered athletes than I already was. With my press credential, I was given access to locker and press rooms for different local pro teams, where I talked with, asked questions of, and made friendships with some of the most high-profile athletes in the country.

It was about this time it began to hit me how differently my childhood was from Adam and Blake's. I grew up in such humble beginnings. The only man of influence I knew was my dad, but even then, the sightings of him were few. I grew up like a buoy that had been cut loose—always adrift. Sure, I had good teachers here and there, and Walt Hoffman was obviously a pivotal person in my life. But my boys grew up with so much more promise all around them. I'm sure it wasn't something they thought about. It was simply all they knew.

Between the pro athletes and heavy hitting business professionals at church, plus their dad's radio gig with all the sports heroes of the day, the backdrop of their lives was filled with powerful people and a plethora of possibilities. But it was just getting started.

When Adam had his skiing accident, the outpouring from the church was incredible. As pro athletes often do, they tap into their power to bring unexpected joy to the face of a sick boy in a hospital. That's why different autographed sports paraphernalia began arriving at Adam's bedside. How many little boys get that? John Werhas was the instigator in all those displays of love and support. It meant so much to Adam and all of us. I am so grateful to John.

Now, after Yorba Linda Friends began to really grow, John's other passion as chaplain for the Dodgers and Angels became too much for his schedule. So, one day he gives me a call. "Mark, I can't be the chaplain to two teams and still give everything I have to the church. How would you like to be the chaplain to the Dodgers for a year?"

Up to that point, it was enough to go to Dodger games from time to time. But now this...being part of the Dodger organization as a chaplain—it was more than a sports and Dodger-crazed kid from Garden Grove could take. *Me? The chaplain to the Dodgers? Are you kidding me?*

When I accepted the role, I suddenly had access to all the Dodgers I could have asked for. I joyfully became friendly with all the players. I wasn't just a visitor to their inner sanctum, but someone who had real, important business there and therefore was welcomed like a part of the team. John and I even flew to the Dodger training camp in Vero Beach, Florida, *the ultimate Dodger fan fantasy*. There, I found myself sitting at the dining room table having meals with Tommy Lasorda, Mike Piazza, and Eric Karos, listening to Tommy tell stories about Frank Sinatra, Milton Berle, and all the Hall of Famers he knew and played with. When I was introduced to Vin Scully, I nearly fell out of my chair—he meant so much to me from as far back as I can remember. To top it off, there, in the locker room, getting ready to go outside and meet the fans, was Sandy Koufax—putting on his jersey, no less. My heart skipped a beat when I saw the #32. Later, I was standing there shaking his hand, smiling and saying my nice-to-meet-you's, thinking to myself, *Nahhhh. This can't be happening.*

Meanwhile, I wondered if Adam and Blake were actually getting it. Did they know what all this meant and what a dream it was? Shouldn't they have been more freaked out about being among baseball royalty? Maybe it takes being a little kid lying on a bed in a tiny, hot house on Oasis Street, listening to the baseball games on a radio to really feel the full magnificence of walking into the Dodger clubhouse, the dugout, and Dodger Stadium from the underbelly. But, when I brought my boys in and out of the Dodger facility, and they jumped around the dugout and hung out behind the scenes, I thought to myself: this is exactly the life I wished I had as a kid. I remember the time when Orel Hershiser shook hands with Adam, and Adam, being just a kid, gave him a limp fish. Orel looked at him and said, "That's not how you give a handshake. Look me in the eye and give it some muscle, like this. Now say, 'It's nice to meet you.'"

I thought to myself, *Am I seeing things, or is my son getting life-instruction from a wonderful, Christian future Hall of Famer like Orel Hershiser?*

It was about this time that I realized how all of this was shaping them, especially Adam. He simply believed that he belonged in such quarters with very accomplished, famous, powerful people—because that's all he knew. Adam held his head high, and talked with everybody young and old as if he was one of them.

He has a confidence and ease about him. He is comfortable in his own skin. He is so different than me.

I remember the time I drove Adam and Blake through the neighborhood of Adam's favorite Anaheim Duck superstar, Teemu Selanne. Teemu had just bought a home in a swank neighborhood and I just happened to know where it was. So, I told them which house it was, and Adam said (not like he had a brilliant idea, but like Teemu might have been expecting him), "Stop the car. I'm going to go up and say hi."

"You're just going to go up to Teemu's house and ring the doorbell?"

Adam looked at me like I just asked the world's most obvious question. "Stop the car," he said.

Adam went up to the house—by himself—and rang the doorbell. Someone came to the door to say that Selanne wasn't there, and Adam returned like he had just been out for a stroll. No big deal. I was impressed. *Get a load of him,* I thought.

The large living never seemed to die down for Adam. He was accepted to Pepperdine University in Malibu overlooking the Pacific Ocean. It's the kind of university that some of the most powerful people in the world send their kids. Kids of professional sports team owners, major movie stars, kids who arrive in L.A. by Lear Jet. Some of the kids he went to school with became stars themselves. Adam, always rather unimpressed, just thought of them as pals.

By the time I was 52, after 25 years of running the company, I began to wonder what the future of MBW would look like.

Would it include me? At that point in Adam's life, he had met with some frustrations in his chosen profession of real estate and had taken a job working in the office at MBW.

Blake also came to work at MBW after he earned his degree from Vanguard University. Blake worked as a job coordinator and was doing stellar work at one of the most difficult positions at MBW. There was only one problem. Blake did not love the work. Ever since he was a little guy, he has had a love for cars, cameras, and design. So, when a job became available to him in the automobile industry, he jumped at it. It's where he was able to use his photography talents, and after a few years there, he was promoted to a position in the Product Development Department. Cars. Cameras. Design. He made the right decision for himself and his family. I respect him a great deal for that decision. He is a man of tremendous faith. Karen and I prayed our sons would find careers that enabled them to know they were using the gifts that God gave them. God answered that prayer, too.

In the meantime, Adam took to the waterproofing business like a duck to water, and I could see he was thriving. Given that Adam is committed to Christ, strong in his faith, a leader, confident in his worth, comfortable in all environments, and educated—something most top guys in construction are not—I considered that it might be the right time to hand him the reins to MBW. It was one of those moments, like so many others in my life, when God orchestrated the pieces, saying yes to a thought in my head.

Whereas I was always way too self-conscious, too inward, to be the kind of leader that gets the most from his people while still giving the most to his people, Adam stepped up into the role in a huge way—as if his whole life directed him here. He does not try to duplicate what I did. Instead, he has forged his own path, creating a new culture and tenor. He seeks the advice of business advisors. He sets aggressive goals and creates action plans to achieve them. He walks into corporate events or business mixers with a strange combination of ease, confidence, and humility, which instantly attracts people to him. He is the perfect representative of MBW. (To provide a final bit of contrast, at one point I actually considered giving one of my employees the use of my name as if he was Mark Beamish, because people thought he was me, anyway. I was too shy to be the constant face of the company and would much rather have a stand-in.)

And this is where the footsteps of God seem to have been leading—here, to the generous heart of Adam. The greatest thing about owning MBW is what it represents for so many people, and in so many ways. And, under Adam's leadership, it will likely mean *so much more*.

> And this is where the footsteps of God seem to have been leading—here, to the generous heart of Adam.

Adam provides his employees with a chaplain so they can have support, encouragement, spiritual guidance and comfort. MBW is deeply immersed in the efforts of the Muscular Dystrophy Association, supporting telethons, summer camps, walk-a-thons and their many drives. MBW has held fundraisers to support the Free Wheel Chair Mission and the Westside Food Bank in Los Angeles. In

2015, they were also on the board for the CureDuchenne: Getzlaf Shootout Golf Tournament. Adam is particularly mindful of the more than 400 family members that stem from the 130 employees (2016) and has helped them in their time of need on many occasions. In fact, he's even forming a committee to increase employee engagement for these initiatives so that he can provide the benefits and blessings to both the receivers and givers. Adam is deeply generous.

I look back at all that has happened, and then gaze forward to all that is taking place, and it brings me to a sense of awe. I am amazed. I am humbled. I am so grateful.

It's still God's company.

FOR REFLECTION

Is your company yours alone? Could it be that God has given it to you, not just to provide for your family, but to do great things for others, those you know and those you'll never know, and never know about? Would that be pleasing to you?

Take a few moments and think about the ways your company might bless others. Are there any actions you can take today that might begin that process? Do you believe a company whose goal it is to bless others is treated differently by God over one that doesn't subscribe to the same?

Epilogue

I LOOKED AT JIM LYING IN HIS HOSPITAL BED fighting to survive the effects of his heart attack, and it was difficult to watch. He had been my right-hand man at MBW since the early days, and now in this tough, new slog of trying to beat back the conditions that threatened his life, I wanted to be there for him. I really care for Jim. He's a good man. I credit him with a lot of the success of MBW.

Frank, his brother and a good friend of mine from way back in the MNBS days, was there caring for his big bro. As we stepped outside Jim's room to talk, Frank asked me a question that took me a bit off guard because it seemed to be so many years removed from anyone's interest. "So, why *did* you hire Jim?"

It took me back 30 years to when MBW was just a few months

old and I saw that I needed somebody to handle the sales part of the business. I knew that after Jim graduated from George Fox University in Oregon, he stayed up there and began working in construction. Jim was a big guy and he had this air of confidence that made me look up to him. It seems like every guy who is older than me and has some authority about him is somebody I look up to—even to this day.

So, I called Jim up and, not knowing one thing more about his abilities other than *he had some construction experience*, I floated the idea of his coming to work for me to take over sales. He made the trip down and we met to talk about the possibilities, but the truth is, none of that mattered. I knew I was going to offer him the job before I ever dialed his number.

When he got back to Oregon, he told his wife, Kathy, that he wanted to take the job with MBW back in Southern California where they are both from. "Is that cool with you?" he asked her.

"Are you kidding?" she said. "I've been praying we'd move back down to California for the last two months."

It's another example of things coming together in a way where God seemed to be orchestrating the events in my life, even though I was merely acting impulsively. But it got me to thinking. How many times did I shoot from the hip and it not work out?

The more I thought about it, the more examples came to mind. In fact, for all the times that things worked out, there might have been just as many that did not.

There were decisions that I made rashly that fell flat and threatened the survival of the business. I lost both relationships and money because of stupid things I did or said without thinking. There were things I quickly bought and never used and there were things I didn't buy and then suffered without. There were people who I hired, then fired, then hired back. And then fired again! And guess what? I hired them again! But of all the impulse moves that I managed to perpetrate on my business, the one that sticks out the most was when I was trying to figure out an exit plan for myself. I was trying to set up a way for me to retire from the business and have Adam step into the top tier. But, how was he going to do that without having that kind of experience?

> Looking back, this idea had oy vey written all over it.

As you might recall, Ed Westbrook, my friend and a professor at Vanguard University, had me talk to his class, and in the process, I came in contact with three of his students who really impressed me. Ed concurred that these were young men with bright futures. Two of them were friends of Floyd's kids and so Floyd knew them and had nice things to say. Suddenly, my mind started churning.

I called the three of them together and revealed my idea. I wanted to groom them to take over MBW as co-partners along with a fourth member, Adam. That way, they could prop each other up and no one person would be thrown into the fire. That's right, my plan for a successful transfer of power was to create a CEO made up of four dudes who had never run a business before.

It seemed like a good idea at the time.

Looking back, this idea had *oy vey* written all over it. How I thought four young guys were going to rise to the top of MBW, a multimillion-dollar business, and do it smoothly and equally is truly a remarkable feat of naivete'. I mean, what could go wrong?

Of course, one of the young men started to assert more power than the others and suddenly the balance sharply tipped. In addition, he was showing a bit of ruthlessness in the way he went about things and suddenly I had a situation on my hands. The last straw was when I got a call from our banker who said, "If he's treating all your vendors the way he's treating me, nobody is going to work with MBW again."

All these relationships, including my banker, had taken years to foster. They had been forged in my name and on goodwill between the both parties. I couldn't have some young guy come in and trash them all. So, I dissolved the four-headed CEO and left Adam leading our small office in San Diego.

After, I looked back at the destruction and thought, "What was I thinking?"

I guess I wasn't.

Other unwise decisions came flooding to my mind as I sat there outside Jim's hospital room with Frank back inside. That's when it occurred to me that God had not been blessing me because of me, but despite me.

EPILOGUE

But why? Why bless me and save my company when I didn't deserve it? When I consider how Jesus works in the lives of others, I see, time and again, that He always drops these mindboggling blessings right into the laps of people who do not deserve them. *By His grace…* that appears to be His M.O.

> His heart was nearly beating out of his chest.

Looking back to the story of the Prodigal Son in Luke 15, what strikes me the most is all the excited, unabashed, slightly undignified freak-out that Jesus has no problem likening His own actions to when the Prodigal Son, who asks for his inheritance only to go off and live a life of debauchery, comes home. The Bible says, "He (the father) was filled with compassion." Another translation reads, "His heart was nearly beating out of his chest." No other king in history blows a joy-gasket when a subject returns. In fact, other kings make an example out of runaways by making them pay dearly. But, Jesus describes Himself as the Master who runs with a full-throttled gallop, exposing his ankles (a no-no back in the day) to attack His son with love, a party and kisses. The son tries to give his ol' dad an "I'm sorry," but the father won't even listen. *His joy won't let Him.*

In Micah 7, it says that God "delights to show mercy." It does not stipulate. I don't have to have my act together. Just ask the ever-flawed Peter after the resurrection of Christ when he denied Jesus three times.

God, in all His expansiveness, is love. Our sins, foibles, weakness, and mistakes are simply no match.

If you ever happen to see me, you'll notice I stand with my heels slightly together, a hand in my pocket and a *Whatever* posture that conveys, *It's all good*. I like to face the sun so I'm always catching as many rays as possible. All my movements are laidback. The way I talk is a bit carefree; even my laugh is a bit breezy. Funny thing is, it's exactly the way I was at age 16. Back then, however, it was because I was a surfer basking in the glow of how cool it was to be me. Today, I'm just basking in the glow of how amazing it is to belong to Jesus, and to be completely under His mercy and grace.

LINKBOOKLEGACIES.COM

Made in the USA
Las Vegas, NV
23 February 2021